# THE
# ASHANTI
# OF
# GHANA

## Also by the same author

# THE
# ASHANTI
# OF
# GHANA

## SONIA BLEEKER

illustrated by Edith G. Singer

**William Morrow and Company**     New York 1966

Grateful recognition
is given to
Dr. Robert A. Lystad,
of Johns Hopkins University,
for reading and criticizing
the manuscript.

Copyright © 1966 by Sonia Bleeker
All rights reserved.
Published simultaneously in Canada
by George J. McLeod Limited, Toronto.
Printed in the United States of America.
Library of Congress Catalog Card Number 66–14751

# TABLE
# OF
# CONTENTS

# 1

## POMP AND SPLENDOR

The Ashanti are a Negroid people who live in the land that is now called Ghana. The men average about five feet five inches in height. The women are shorter, averaging little more than five feet. Men and women are usually slender, and they have a dark skin, broad nose, and a long head.

Although clothing is not a necessity in this hot, humid country, men and women took great pride in the old days in wearing elaborate clothing. They spent much time weaving and caring for their garments, and weaving became an outstanding Ashanti craft.

The Ghana of today was once divided into three parts. The northern region, or top of the country, was called Northern Territories. It was well known to the Ashanti and for centuries was crisscrossed by traders to the lands of the

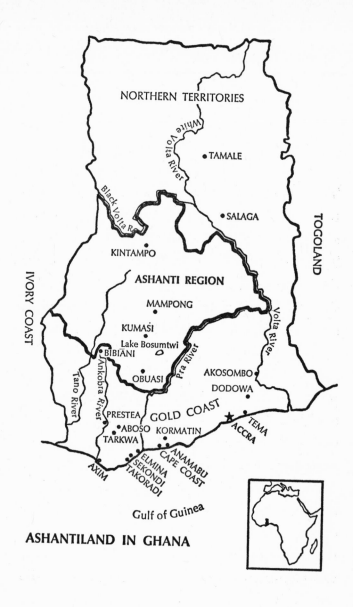

NORTHERN TERRITORIES

White Volta River

● TAMALE

● SALAGA

Black Volta R.

KINTAMPO

**ASHANTI REGION**

MAMPONG

KUMASI

Lake Bosumtwi

● BIBIANI

OBUASI

Pra River

AKOSOMBO
DODOWA

Volta River

IVORY COAST

Tano River

Ankobra River

PRESTEA    GOLD COAST

● ABOSO    KORMATIN

TARKWA                              ★ ACCRA    TEMA

ELMINA    ANAMABU
SEKONDI    CAPE COAST
TAKORADI

AXIM

TOGOLAND

Gulf of Guinea

**ASHANTILAND IN GHANA**

Ashanti. Some of these African and Arabian traders came from the Sudan, and some came all the way across the Sahara Desert from the Mediterranean coast.

The southern region consisted of a narrow strip of coastline and was known as the Gold Coast. About twenty miles inland the grasslands and thick growth of bush near the coast of the Gulf of Guinea changed into dense hilly tropical forest. This forest farther north gave way to dry grasslands that stretched for miles and miles. The grasslands finally merged with the sands of the Sahara Desert. Through the country ran the great Volta River.

In this center region lived the Ashanti. It is believed that the Ashanti, like the rest of the tribes in this part of Africa, farmed the land. But they could not have survived on their farming alone. It has been said that most West Africans in the early days rarely had enough to eat.

The Ashanti raised a cereal called guinea corn (also known as sorghum or durra), which can only be grown in areas of moderate rainfall.

Too much rain or too little killed the crop. They may also have grown another cereal called millet and a kind of rice. They probably had edible yams, which are a tuberous root crop, unlike sweet potatoes, even though we sometimes call our sweet potatoes yams. The Ashanti may have used many kinds of wild plants, which the women gathered, but new crops are now so firmly established that the useful old plants have been forgotten. The West Africans also used the fat of the palm seed—palm oil. They made a fermented drink (palm wine, sometimes called palm toddy in America) from the sap of the palms.

The Ashanti could not domesticate cattle, however, because their land was in the midst of the tsetse fly belt. The tsetse-borne diseases infect and kill cattle the moment they near the forest area. Wild animals seem to be immune, and to some extent sheep and goats. Most Ashanti must have depended in the old days on hunting to get food containing proteins and fats. The weapons that they used were bows and arrows or spears and clubs. They also developed rather ingenious traps.

The Ashanti usually hunted in pairs. Two men entered the forest, selected a big tree close to an animal trail, and hid behind it. They waited patiently till they saw a movement among the tree trunks. One hunter called out, his hand over his mouth, Indian fashion. The curious animal left its hiding place, moving timidly and cautiously toward the caller. Then the hunters killed it. The men waited for the next animal to appear. When they had sufficient meat they returned home.

Another hunting method was to form a group. Men told one another about the planned hunt and selected a leader, an older and experienced hunter. On the day set for the hunt the men gathered in the center of the village, under the village assembly tree. Usually they brought their small sons and nephews. These youngsters came unarmed. They followed their relative to watch and learn. The hunters were dressed in their oldest garments and carried clubs, and bows and arrows. Each man wore all the charms for hunting that he owned, hanging either from his neck in a tooled leather pouch or tucked into an armlet. Charms not only brought the hunter good luck, they also kept disaster away.

The group always left for the hunt early in the morning. The men and boys followed the leader in single file into the forest. At this time of day the forest was filled with a blue mist and the narrow path was barely visible. After walking for about an hour, the party arrived at a crossing of the trails. There the leader divided the hunters into two groups. Half of the men with the weapons and all the unarmed youths went off in one direction. After waiting for a while, having given them a head start, the rest of the group went in the opposite direction.

The tropical forest was always dark, cool, and moist in the mornings. The sun could not penetrate because the trees branched high overhead, forming thick crowns. There was, therefore, very little undergrowth. The massive old trunks were covered with mosses and lichens. However, because there was no undergrowth, visibility was about 100 yards and in some places even more.

Barefoot, the men walked noiselessly over the damp ground. The fallen twigs were so wet that they did not crackle underfoot. The leader signaled a halt. Each man chose a tree for cover, so that suddenly the group of hunters melted into the forest and disappeared. There was complete silence now. No movement of any kind. The forest, of course, teemed with animals and birds, and the hunters knew that they were being watched.

After a while the beaters in the first group began to drum. The drumming was followed by cautious whistling and calls. A shot was released. In an instant the hushed forest filled with life. Dull-colored shadows began to move in the distance. Soon men were able to distinguish squirrels, blue guinea fowls, and francolins—a kind of partridge—on the ground. Birds flew overhead. Small antelopes—several yellow-backed duikers and blue duikers—appeared. They stopped and listened to the noise. The men in the second party shot their weapons, and the animals crumpled to the ground. As quickly as the hunt started, it was over.

The hunters walked over to pick up the animals. They were lucky to get this much game in one morning. After eating some of the meat and some of the biscuits called *canky* that they had brought along, they sent the rest of the meat back to the village and moved on. The hunters were prepared to stay in the forest for several days, or for as long as a week if necessary.

People also went into the forest to hunt for snails, which were a favorite and nourishing food. Men, women, and children all joined in such a hunt. The tree snails in their shell were about the size of a man's fist, and they lived and fed on tree trunks. They did not harm the tree, since they ate the lichens that covered the trunks rather than the leaves.

The best time to collect snails was at the beginning of the rainy season in May or in August, because the wet trunks caused the snails to move in search of more succulent lichens. The snail hunting season lasted for about six weeks, and the Ashanti erected temporary shelters of twigs and leaves, so they could remain in the forest for the duration.

The people collected the snails in large baskets, which they brought with them. Each person had to make several trips back to camp to empty the filled baskets. At the camp women built small fires for drying and smoking the snails. A woman cracked the snail shell between two paddles and dropped the soft meat into a basket. Another woman strung the meat on long wooden skewers, about 100 snails to a skewer. She placed the skewers near the fire to dry.

When dried, the skewers were moved to trays for smoking. The fires under the smoking trays were kept going all day. The snails, dried and smoked, were thus preserved. The women then tied the snails into bundles of twenty skewers, so that two bundles held about four thousand snails and made up a load of sixty pounds. That was the average load one person carried out of the forest.

Snail hunting had to be regulated by the chiefs. There was always the fear that if the Ashanti took too many snails out of the forest they might exhaust the supply. In some years snail hunting was forbidden altogether. But when scouts assured the chief that the snails were plentiful, he permitted his people to hunt them.

Fish was also a very important source of needed protein in the diet of the Ashanti. There were rivers and streams that yielded fish, and the only large lake in Ashantiland, Lake Bosumtwi, supplied ample fish for the villages that grew up along its shores.

This lake is about four miles wide and covers

some thirteen square miles. It is situated in a hollow—a depression with steep sides that rise between 600 and 700 feet. It has a proven depth of some 250 feet and an estimated depth of 500 feet. Surrounding streams flow into Bosumtwi, but there is no outflow. Still its waters remain fresh. Once it was believed that the lake was of volcanic origin, but now scientists think that the land subsided and gradually filled with rainwater.

A remarkable occurrence of Lake Bosumtwi is that once a year there is a sudden explosion in the lake followed by a stench of rotten eggs. Thousands upon thousands of fish are thrust to the surface and die. The Ashanti are quick to collect this rich harvest, which they believe the lake spirit has given them to eat.

Scientists have explained this phenomenon by saying that the explosion is due to organic matter that grows, collects, and rots on the muddy lake bottom. It becomes so buoyant with gases that accumulate as it rots that it rises to the surface in a black scum. Since Lake Bosumtwi has no outlet, the scum is not carried away.

Instead, some of the gas that it gives off causes it to ignite instantaneously as it comes into contact with the atmosphere, accounting for the little lights that the Ashanti report seeing all over the lake at night.

Due to these occurrences the Ashanti became convinced long ago that spirits lived in the lake, and they made sacrifices of fowl, eggs, palm wine, a cow, sheep, or a dog to them. The place of sacrifice, which the chiefs and the priests approached with bare feet and shoulders, was a sacred rock. There they asked the spirit to come

and eat the meat and drink the wine, which they sprinkled over the stone. They prayed that he give life to the chief, to the Ashanti nation, and to all the people present.

Because they believed a powerful spirit lived in the center of Lake Bosumtwi, no Ashanti ever swam out to the center or took a raft there. No canoes, paddles, or brass pans were permitted in the water. No fishhooks could be used to catch the fish.

Men and women did swim near the shores of the lake, however. They used special wide planks, which they called *paduas*. A man lay on his stomach on the *padua* and paddled himself along with his hands. He used his feet, too, in a kind of flutter to steer the *padua*. As a result of these customs, the Ashanti became excellent swimmers of great endurance. A man could paddle his *padua* for as long as eight hours at a time. The men took passengers on rafts, made up of two *paduas* lashed together. They propelled these rafts by pushing them with other *paduas*.

Since no fishhooks were permitted, the Ashanti wove special kinds of nets for catching fish. They submerged them, and when the net was filled with fish, the men dived under it and brought it up. Then they put the catch into wooden bowls and baskets and carried it away.

By the end of the eighteenth century the Ashanti were at their mightiest—in wealth and territory. At this time the English received permission to come to Kumasi, the Ashanti capital. This visit to Kumasi took place in 1810, and we have an eyewitness account of it.

The Englishman who described the visit was T. Edward Bowdich. He wrote that Kumasi was surrounded by a marsh to protect it. The marsh was forty yards wide and three feet deep. After Bowdich and his party crossed the marsh on foot, the king's messengers came to tell them to rest awhile, since the king was making preparations to meet them.

As they neared the capital and the people saw them, the English were greeted with music and volley after volley from the muskets of Ashanti warriors. It seemed to the Englishmen that a hundred bands, each using drums, horns, flutes, rattles, and gongs, were all sounding at the same time, each playing a different tune. They were right in this observation, since every Ashanti chief had his own band, and it played his songs and tunes. Men and boys waved small flags, which they had evidently acquired in trade from various European countries. Thousands of people—civilians and an estimated 30,-000 warriors—lined up all along the miles of roads. The Ashanti were as curious and as eager to see the Europeans, whom few of them had seen at that time, as the Europeans were to see the Ashanti.

It was getting toward midday and the sun was unbearably hot. The broad, clean streets of Kumasi were bordered with spreading banyan trees, offering shade and relief from the dust that the people and the dancers had kicked up. Rows of houses ran along the streets on both sides. The peaked roofs were thatched and extended well over the walls of the houses, thus providing more shade.

The houses gave the impression of being two-storied. Actually they consisted of a single story, which rested on a floor that was sometimes as high as six feet above street level. The floors were made of packed clay—a highly polished red ochre—and red ochre steps led up to them. Around the base were carved decorations. The front of each house was wide open to the street, so that the two side walls and the back wall formed a sort of porch. Openings in the back wall led to the private family rooms. The houses were built of adobe, plastered and washed with white clay. They all looked clean and trim.

The front rooms were crowded with women and children who were trying to get a glimpse of the visitors and watch the festivities. When the Englishmen reached the side streets, they noted that the houses there were also filled with people. Rows upon rows of heads eagerly turned in their direction and watched them pass.

The English had to move slowly. They were stopped by groups of dancers, who twirled, leaped, and plunged before them, in brilliant, elaborate, and rich costumes. The captains, or leaders, of the dancers wore headdresses with gilded horns in the front, trailing long eagles' feathers on the sides. Each headdress was covered with cowrie shells, and it was held in place with a band tied under the chin. At one time cowrie shells were the only kind of money that the Ashanti and many other Africans used, and so the shells were extremely valuable.

The dancers wore a red cloth vest, ornate

with gold. On their wide sash were attached fine pouches, brass bells, horns, animal tails, and all sorts of shells and knives. Each of the leaders had a long leopard tail attached in the back to his sash. Their cotton trousers were wide and very loose, and their soft, red leather boots reached halfway up the thigh. The boots were attached to the wide sash with small gold chains. Trousers and boots were elaborately fringed and decorated with horses' tails. A small quiver of poisoned arrows hung from each man's right wrist, and he carried a small spear in a red sheath in his left hand. Between his teeth he held a long iron chain. Iron at the time was valued by the Ashanti, since it was hard to obtain and therefore scarce.

The warriors, too, were dressed up. Their face and arms were painted with long white lines. These streaks against their jet black skin looked like armor. They wore leather aprons and wide belts. Numerous small gourds filled with gunpowder, brass bells, shells, and small pouches hung from their belt. They carried clusters of knives in sheaths, iron chains, and collars. Their muskets lay on leopard-skin rests.

The English finally reached the Kumasi marketplace, which covered almost a mile in circumference. It was packed with people, some standing, some sitting on stools, and some sitting on the ground. The warriors could not move to make room for the Europeans as they passed. Bowdich stepped on their feet and was ready to apologize, but the warriors didn't mind, for their feet were tough. So Bowdich proceeded toward the center, where the king and his elaborate retinue awaited the European delegation, amidst the noise of the bands, which now played even more vigorously. Every now and then the music stopped, and the silence was a great relief. Only the flutes continued a plaintive air. To the English these instruments sounded as pleasant as Scottish bagpipes.

The chiefs, moving about under huge umbrellas held by umbrella carriers, were a dazzling sight, too. Their gold breastplates, crescents, chains, and bracelets shimmered in the sun. The carriers swirled their umbrellas and swung them up and down in a sort of umbrella dance. Hundreds of these umbrellas bobbed up and down. Each was covered with red and yellow silks, with fringes, scallops, and mirrors. The gold crescents atop the umbrellas were skillfully worked by Ashanti goldsmiths and carvers in the shape of birds and animals. Some umbrellas were covered with leopard skins and mounted with stuffed animals. In the rear of the marketplace was a line of hammocks, which looked like long cradles, and they spilled over with silks and cushions embroidered with gold and beads. The chiefs were carried in them.

Now the greetings began. First each chief shook hands with each of the visitors, so the Englishmen had to stop before every chief's group to exchange greetings. The chiefs wore robes thrown across one shoulder like a Roman toga, leaving the other shoulder bare. These togas were made of narrow strips of silk cloth called *kente* made by skillful Ashanti weavers. Narrow gold bands encircled the chiefs' heads. In addition to the gold breastplate, many wore gold necklaces, intricately designed by their village goldsmiths, and Arab charms. Gold bands as well as strings of beads encircled their knees and ankles. Their soft sandals of green, red, and white leather were ornamented with gold figurines; their arms and wrists were decorated with bracelets. Some had nuggets of gold hanging from their wrists. Many were so heavily laden with bracelets and rings that their arms rested on the shoulders of young retainers. Everywhere were gold pipes and canes. Boys held gold swords with handles formed of heavy casts of animals' heads.

The Englishmen finally reached his majesty. He was surrounded by four attendants, called linguists or spokesmen. They spoke for the king and also acted as his interpreters and advisers. The king did not speak directly to people; the linguist spoke for him. In addition to their rich dress, the spokesmen carried gold canes. Behind them stood the keeper of the treasury, holding his tools of office: gold boxes containing gold dust, scales for weighing gold, and a trayful of gold weights. These weights were also cast into animals and insects of many kinds, shapes, and sizes, worked with supreme skill. The palace

cook was also there, surrounded by covered gold and copper utensils. In front of the king, under a separate umbrella standing on an elephant hide, was the dazzling golden stool that the Ashanti worshiped. In their beliefs the ancient stool represented the souls of the great ancestors of their king and of all the people. It was carefully guarded by its carriers.

The king, sitting on a carved stool placed on leopard skins, extended his hand to Bowdich in greeting. He was a man in his late thirties, somewhat stout, but with a very kind face. His toga was made of a dark green silk. A pointed diadem was painted in white on his forehead, and his shoulders and chest also had white ornaments, which resembled flowers, painted on them. His headband was of aggery shells and shiny stone beads, carved by Ashanti jewelers. From a red silk cord on his right shoulder were suspended three large sapphires set in gold. The king's arms and hands were covered with gold bracelets and rings. On his knees and ankles were more aggery beads, gold bands, and clusters of gold ornaments of the finest workmanship: tiny drums, stools, guns, and birds. Even his sandals of white leather were embossed across the instep with small sapphires in gold settings.

With a pair of gold castanets attached to his thumb and forefinger the king signaled for silence. The guards behind him kept watch on the crowd and the Englishmen. In the silence that followed, only the fans of the elephant tails could be heard swishing on their ivory handles, and the large ostrich-plume fans created an agreeable breeze.

After the greetings a messenger led the Englishmen under the shade of a tree. They were glad to sit down and rest. It had been a long hot day. The sun was setting. People were turning toward their homes. It grew dark and very quiet. The Englishmen were able to relax.

Suddenly the silence was broken again by drums, horns, and flutes. The king came to bid them good-night before retiring. His procession was preceded by torches. The golden vessels that held the oil in which the boy torch carriers dipped their torches gleamed in the dark. The king was accompanied by his sisters and the older women of the court, each wearing rows of fine gold chains, which also gleamed in the dark.

The visitors were then led to a house allotted them for the visit. Drums kept talking long into the night, presumably keeping people all over the land advised of what had happened on this memorable day—when the capital of the Ashanti welcomed visitors from across the seas.

# 2

# TALKING DRUMS

At the reception in Kumasi the Englishmen noticed three kinds of drums. Small drums hung on red sashes from drummers' necks. Medium-sized drums rested on men's heads, and two drummers stood alongside the drum carrier, beating the drum. Pairs of very large kettle-drums rested on the ground. These were the talking drums. One drummer was assigned to each pair of talking drums. Bells and specially shaped iron pieces were attached to his wrists; they jingled and rang with each drumbeat.

These African talking drums were used for news broadcasts in Africa. They had the reputation of carrying news from one end of the continent to the other. In the 1920's a British anthropologist, Captain R. S. Rattray, was taught how to drum by an Ashanti drummer. Rattray said that he learned to sound the drums

in the same way that a child learns to read words and phrases by sounding them. From childhood Africans also learn the drummed sound of words and phrases. A pattern of tones represents an entire word or an entire phrase.

Captain Rattray, who knew the Ashanti

people and their language (called Akan) very well, was impressed by the talking drums, because everyone around him understood their messages perfectly. Working in the fields, the orchards, or in the courtyard in front of their home, people listened to the daily news broadcasts on the talking drums. Rattray learned that the drummers "spell" out phrases. One drum has a higher pitch than the other. The two drums together imitate the higher and lower tones used by Africans (and by ourselves) in pronouncing words. A phrase is played on both drums and is followed by a pause. Like all things that are paired, the Africans refer to the two drums as male and female.

Captain Rattray soon began to relate the drumming to the manner in which the Africans speak. He noted that they gesture as they speak with an up-and-down movement of the hands, as though they were drumming. Not only the Ashanti, but most Africans when they talk wave their arms and then bring them down sharply. The drummer, imitating these hand gestures, beats the drum with the same emphasis. His stops and pauses may be looked upon as commas and periods in our sentences.

An Ashanti does not often recognize single words in his language, as we do in ours. We know the individual words in English, because we have been taught to read single words. Even when we think, we are aware of how each single word should be written. A very young child, however, does not think in single words. He thinks in phrases and repeats them together: goodnight; Igotosleep; breadandbutter; ice-creamcone.

All Ashanti, like ourselves, learn their language in this way. Until fifty years ago, however, most Ashanti did not know how to read or write, so they did not learn single words as we do. People speak in phrases, which to them sound like one word. "I am going" to them is a group of sounds with the meaning to go. Were you to ask a nonliterate Ashanti for the meaning of a single word, he might be unable to answer. But he could readily understand and explain the meaning of a group of words, which are used frequently.

When listening to the talking drums, the people hear a number of beats with a pause before and after. These beats correspond to a spoken phrase or sentence. Through constant repetition from childhood, these drummed phrases become as familiar to them as common tunes are to us. A person does not have to strain to listen to each drumbeat. He automatically understands a group of familiar tones.

And so a message can be flashed by the talking drums from one end of the Ashantiland to the other. In the days of Ashanti wars, men on a hunt or working in the fields were alerted by the drums. They would say, "*A-san-te, mo n-ka n-to-a. Ber-a, ber-a!*" (Ashanti, get your powder belts. Come, come!) Although said to be a gross exaggeration, it has been reported that a message relayed through a series of drummers, stationed throughout the land over a distance of 200 miles, reached the warriors faster than a modern telegraphic message could be transmitted. Warriors grabbed muskets and powder belts and rushed to assemble in the center of the village.

There are some ten vowels in the Ashanti language, and the drums can transmit the tone of each vowel. The Ashanti are able to state in the drum language even such fine distinctions as *o-ba* (he comes), *wa-ba* (he has come), *o-re-be-ba* (he is about to come), and the imperative, *ber-a* (come).

Drumming phrases can also describe a person in a general way. When a stranger is seen in Ashanti lands, the drummers notify the people: *o-ba* (he comes). He is tall. He walks or he is carried. The drummers might add some gossip about the purpose of the stranger's visit. An Ashanti chief, before he sets out on a journey to visit a neighboring chief, has his drummer give the particulars of his departure, his expected time of arrival, and the number of people in his party.

Since talking drums transmit sounds and phrases in the Ashanti language, they cannot be understood by those speaking different African languages. However, if a drummer of a neighboring tribe knows Akan, he can readily translate the news he hears into his own language or dialect. If the drummer's language is also based on tones, he can transmit the message on his drums easily. Nevertheless, it is an exaggeration to say that talking drums can send information from one end of the African continent to the other. There are hundreds of languages and dialects in Africa, any of which may form a language barrier that will stop a message. Many Africans speak several dialects of neighboring groups, as well as more than one or two neighboring languages. But most people do not know languages of their more distant neighbors.

It is also easier to send a message than to receive it. Drums transmit only tones, numbers of syllables with pauses for punctuation. Actual vowels or consonants are not transmitted. However, Ashanti drummers have a set of phrases that they constantly use and that are, therefore, familiar to all trained drummers. So long as a drummer sticks to the familiar, he is sure to be understood. When he introduces new phrasing, he may or may not be understood at first. Eventually he will be. In time, a new phrase or phrases will, through repetition, become part of the receivers' vocabulary.

The usual familiar phrases are the naming of a particular chief or a warning of danger. An enemy is approaching; there is a fire in a village, a death; the Europeans or other traders are coming; men are summoned to arms; war is declared.

There is drumming in all Ashanti ceremonies. The drums repeat to the people the history connected with the ceremony. Poetry and legends are also transmitted by the drums.

These large drums, therefore, keep people informed in many different ways. Only chiefs have the right to own the talking drums. Even though women hold high positions among the Ashanti, no woman chief may own drums. Nor may a woman become a drummer.

The order to make a talking drum comes directly from the chief. This order is usually accompanied by gifts to be used to appease the *sumsum* (the spirit) of the tree from which the drum is to be made. The gifts are usually a fowl with curly feathers, eggs, and palm wine, and gold dust is given to each of the craftsmen.

The craftsmen get themselves ready. Taking some food along, they set out into the forest to look for a particular cedar tree from which the drum is to be made. The cedar is not a benevolent tree. Its *sumsum* does not have the reputation of doing good to people. So the chopping down of the cedar is beset with great danger from the very start. The craftsmen fear the tree. Its spirit may seek revenge, because it has been cut down. After selecting a cedar that has a trunk of the right thickness, the craftsman smashes an egg against the trunk and prays:

> I am going to cut you down and carve you.
> Receive this egg and eat.
> Let me be able to cut you and carve you.
> Do not let the ax cut me.
> Do not let me suffer.

Palm wine is poured over the tree before it is chopped. After the tree is cut, the fowl is killed and its flesh placed upon the stump, to further appease the cedar's *sumsum*.

The craftsmen then begin to hollow out the

log. They remain in the forest till the job is done. After sprinkling more palm wine and egg over log and stump, they pray again. "We are taking you to the village. Let the village prosper."

In the village another fowl is killed and its flesh put on the hollowed-out log, and more wine is sprinkled over it. And again the men pray. "Partake of this fowl and wine. Now that we have brought you home, let the village prosper. Do not have us take you to a funeral."

Work on the drum continues. The skin for the mouth of the drum is taken from an elephant's ear. With the hairy side on top, the moistened skin is stretched to overlap the mouth of the drum and tied around with rope. The men curl the edges around the rope, lace another rope through the sides of the skin, and peg it to the ground. As they pull the lacing tight, the skin tightens till it yields the desired pitch.

The pegs and the two drumstick handles to be used for this drum are whittled from a special tree. The handles are wrapped in cloth or covered with rubber to keep them from slipping in the drummer's hands. A drummer fears to let a drumstick slip. He might thus make a mistake in phrasing.

Iron rings are attached to the drum, if it is to be a male drum. (The female drum never has iron rings.) Their jingle gives off a discordant note. The drummers say that the iron rings help the drum to speak well. Rattray believed that the added jingle helps in transmitting consonant sounds.

Next the drum maker ties a white ribbon to the drum. This cloth is also a gift from the chief. As the drum maker puts the cloth around the drum he prays in his chief's name. "Drum, here is a cloth. I am dressing you with it that you may grant me a prosperous reign. Let me be blessed with good health."

The finished drum is not yet ready to use. First eyes must be cut into the drum with more prayers and more offerings. Ever after, before a drummer begins, he says a prayer and makes an offering to the drum's *sumsum*.

At all times drumming is most carefully

done. A drummer dare not "speak" a wrong phrase for fear of punishment from his chief. An error is a great offense to the drum. A fine of a sheep may be imposed upon the drummer for such a mistake. If he persists in making mistakes, his ear may be cut off. The relationship between the drum and its drummer is so close and so personal that a drummer may not teach his son how to drum. He may only teach his nephew. Among the Ashanti a man's sons are not related as closely to him as are his nephews and nieces—that is, his sister's children. Should a father teach his own son to drum, he will die as soon as the boy perfects the art of drumming.

The Ashanti believe that drummers are sacred people. They have been given their talent by the Creator. When the Creator made men, he first created a messenger (the herald) to the chief. Then he created a drummer. In court ceremonies, therefore, the herald is first and stands next to the chief's stool. The drummer stands next to the herald.

A drummer never carries his own drums. They are carried for him, and they are always placed behind the chief while he holds court. At the chief's orders the drummer transmits the news to the assembled people. Before he begins drumming, he pours a few drops of palm wine or rum into the eye of the drum and prays to it.

Rattray's friend, an Ashanti chief, ordered two talking drums for Rattray, so he could learn drumming. The drums were made by the craftsmen according to custom and brought to Rattray's cabin. Rattray then invited an old man, the court drummer, to teach him. When the old drummer arrived he examined the two drums—the male and female. They were standing side by side as was proper—the male drum on the left, the female on the right. "These drums are not yet ready," he said. "They have no eyes. Has any offering been made to them in your house?"

Rattray asked the old man to perform the ceremony. The old drummer cut a small square on the left-hand side of the male drum and two diagonal lines on the right-hand side of the female drum. Having given the drums their eyes, the old man asked for wine and eggs.

Rattray had no wine, but the whisky he had was accepted. The drummer sprinkled some whisky over the eyes and prayed. Then he rubbed one broken egg over the eye of the male drum, the other egg over the eye of the female drum.

Rattray completed the offerings by giving the drummer a fowl for his personal use. The drummer then picked up the drumsticks, ready to begin. Rattray found the lessons absorbing and became good friends with his teacher. With the chief's consent and that of the queen mother, the old man told the history of his clan on the drums and let Rattray record it on a tape recorder. By this time Rattray's vocabulary on the talking drums must have been considerable to be able to understand so much.

To prove how effective talking drums were, Rattray thought it a good idea to introduce the language of the drums to European boy scouts. He felt that drumming would enable boy scouts to speak over longer distances than they could with a semaphore or flag system. When using these methods, the transmitter and receiver had to be within sight of each other. Talking drummers, however, did not need to see each other. Accordingly, Rattray asked an English-speaking African boy scout to drum for him using the Morse code. The African boy used the male drum for the dashes and the female drum for the dots. Over a mile away, through dense Ashanti forest, a European boy scout received the message. He easily understood every word transmitted to him.

# 3

## THE
## GOLDEN
## STOOL

Legends of creation and of men emerging from underground are told by peoples all over the world. The Ashanti, too, have such a legend. Originally they came from the north and spread over their lands in West Africa. From the tribes who had been living there and whom the Ashanti undoubtedly pushed out and replaced, they may have learned their legend of creation.

The legend says that on a Monday night, very long ago, a worm bored its way up to the surface of the earth. Eight men and five women, a dog, and a leopard followed the worm. At first the people were so astounded by what they saw that they looked about them with fear. But the first ancestor, Adu Ogyinae, soothed the frightened people by putting his hands on their shoulders.

The people immediately began to gather

branches and leaves for building huts. Two days later the first tragedy beset them: a tree fell and killed Adu Ogyinae. He died on a Wednesday, which thus became a sacred day. The people were left alone and hungry, without a leader. However, the dog brought them a burning twig. The people put food upon the fire, cooked it, and gave it to the dog to eat. When the food did not harm the dog, the people ate it too and liked it.

Eventually they built up a settlement. The people took on a clan name of Aduana. Their population grew and was divided into six groups named Atwae, Abrade, Ada, Amoakwade, Amanwere, and Nyampasakyi. Each of these ancestors claimed descent from an animal —the frog, parrot, bat, crow, buffalo, mole— which became their totem animal. Clan members of such a totem do not hunt the animal or eat its flesh.

To commemorate the eight male ancestors who emerged from underground, the Ashanti buried eight pots at the spot in a grove that is now held sacred. The king of the Ashanti sent a cow each year to be sacrificed at this spot. Some of the meat was placed in the pots to feed the ancestral spirits. Forty years ago the sacred grove was located near Kumasi. Today the city has grown and spread so that the grove is within city limits.

The sacredness of the grove is such that any person accused of a crime who flees there must not be punished. Should the king insist on having him captured, it is said that something terrible will happen to him before the year is over.

The supreme god of the Ashanti is Nyankopon, the sky god. No image is ever made of him, although images of lesser gods sometimes appear. The other gods are many. Their spirits are in rivers, in rocks, in trees, flowers, animals —in everything that exists on the earth and in the sky.

The head of a family on presenting to the chief a sheep and wine to honor the spirits of the dead can get special permission to be buried under the floor of his sleeping room. Then his successor (usually his nephew) will place his sleeping mat on the floor over the grave. There he will sleep in comfort, knowing that his spirit ancestor watches over him.

The dead are constantly in the thoughts of the living. Unlike many people the world over, who fear the dead, the Ashanti feel secure in the presence of their ancestral spirits. At the beginning of a meal men and women put a morsel of food and a few drops of water or wine on the ground for the spirits, called *samanfo*. When an Ashanti dies, he is sure that his family will always think of him, pray to him, and give him food.

After an illness an Ashanti says, "I thank the *samanfo*." No business transaction is considered finished until a few drops of wine have been sprinkled on the ground to thank the ancestors. The land, which produces everything, belongs to the ancestors. Sacrifices are made to the *samanfo* at the installation of a chief, when a marriage is agreed upon, when it takes place, and at the birth of a child. When a man is about to die, the priest comforts him with the explanation that the *samanfo* are calling for him. To a dying widow he might say, "You have been thinking of your dead husband daily. Now his *samanfo* at last calls you to join him." Should an infant die, the Ashanti believe that it belonged to the spirits. The spirit mother may have wanted to go someplace and so parted from her child for a few days. Such a child is not even mourned by its parents, since it was not intended permanently for this earth.

The golden stool is the Ashanti symbol of ancestor worship. A priest who lived in the eighteenth century, named Okomfo Anokye, was the Ashanti hero who helped get the stool for the people. Legends have grown around both. Since a people's beliefs are very real to them, it is now hard to separate historic facts from legend.

The golden stool has come to represent Ashanti nationhood and well being—their *sumsum*. Belief has it that should the golden stool ever be taken from the Ashanti or destroyed, the Ashanti nation will die out.

The golden stool, as the Ashanti old men tell, came from the heavens. At that time, early in the eighteenth century, the king of Kumasi was Osai Tutu. He was the fourth king of the Ashanti—fearless and wise. Legend has it that while Osai Tutu was visiting a city on the coast, he found Okomfo Anokye tied to a log. Anokye was then a young man filled with wanderlust. He had been traveling for some years gathering wisdom from old men and priests all over West Africa. Somehow he was accused of a misdemeanor and punished by the chief of the city. Osai Tutu pleaded with the chief and Anokye was freed. This favor Anokye never forgot, and in return made Osai Tutu a great king. Anokye had acquired supernatural powers by that time. People no longer called him only Anokye. They added Okomfo, meaning priest, magician, and prophet, to his name.

While still traveling, Okomfo Anokye preached that the sky god had told him the Ashanti would become a great nation, provided they united under Osai Tutu. This prophecy reached Kumasi even before Anokye returned. When he did, a council of state with all the Ashanti chiefs was ready for his reception. King

Osai Tutu presided with the queen mother beside him.

Okomfo Anokye began to pray. There was a rumbling in the skies. A black cloud appeared and slowly began to descend upon the assembled people. The cloud with white, thick dust trailing it wove its way among the chiefs, landed in Osai Tutu's lap, and dissolved. It left a wooden stool covered with gold. The golden stool never touched earth, and it has not touched the earth for the two and a half centuries since its legendary arrival. It always rests on an elephant hide.

The golden stool stands on a square base, and the seat is supported by three curved legs. No one ever actually sits on the golden stool, even when a ceremony calls for the king's taking possession of it. Instead, he bends his knees and pretends that he is sitting down while his attendants hold him up. No king has ever *sat* down; the stool is too sacred. Always, during ceremonies, the golden stool is carried by its own attendants under its own huge umbrella, and it is covered with a specially woven cloth.

In the days of Osai Tutu a people called the

Denkera, whose warriors had defeated the Ashanti, lived to the southwest. At the time of the stool's appearance the king sent a messenger to Kumasi demanding the annual tribute. The messenger arrived carrying a large bowl that in the past the Ashanti had been made to fill with gold. He also demanded that each chief send his king a favorite wife and favorite son.

Emboldened by Okomfo Anokye's presence, one of the chiefs struck the messenger and killed him. Instead of the gold, Anokye poured the messenger's blood into the bowl. Each Ashanti chief dipped a finger into the bowl and swore to fight the Denkera. The talking drums immediately announced war, and each chief summoned his warriors.

Despite his great supernatural powers, Okomfo Anokye took no chances on the favorable outcome of the war. He changed himself into a beautiful maiden and sat down in the marketplace in the town of Denkera to sell fish. As planned, the king's men spotted the beautiful maiden and promptly brought her to the palace to become the king's wife. While the king slept,

Anokye removed his heart and took it back to Kumasi with him. A stool was being built for Osai Tutu, and Anokye had the Denkera's brave heart buried inside the stool to add more power to Osai Tutu.

The Denkera were routed, of course. Their king had no heart for the fighting and sat under a tree with one of his many wives during the battle. The Ashanti found him and beheaded him. The king of Denkera's gold chains were added as decorations for the golden stool.

Okomfo Anokye influenced battle after battle and led his people to victory. Each time he performed the necessary magic and advised the warriors how to behave. To insure victory, they usually fasted while fighting. Whenever anyone broke a fast, the Ashanti lost a battle. The warrior who was the cause of the defeat usually paid for it with his life. Many, many legends of Okomfo Anokye's deeds are known to the Ashanti and repeated by one generation to another. He is their greatest hero.

As Anokye was aging, he began to worry about finding a way to defeat death and so achieve eternal life for himself and his people. For this search, Anokye left Kumasi and set out on a journey once again. He told the Ashanti that he would be away for seven years and seventy-seven days and nights. No one need mourn for him during this time, nor fire guns in his honor, nor weep. He would be sure to return. With this message he stepped into his home and closed the door.

For seven years and seventy-seven days and nights a guard walked in front of Anokye's hut. When the time was up, a nephew ordered the hut opened, expecting to find his uncle inside. No one was there. A period of nation-wide mourning was declared immediately. Just as the weeping started an old man, some distance from Kumasi, approached an Ashanti farmer and asked why the sudden weeping and firing of guns. Our Anokye is dead, he was told. The old man exclaimed, "But I am Okomfo Anokye. As you can see I am alive."

No one saw Anokye afterward. He must have been disappointed that his people failed to obey his instructions and so decided not to return.

The eternal life, which he had found, was thus never brought to his people.

In the decades that followed the Ashanti continued victorious in war after war. The golden stool was carried into each of these battles. Although the Ashanti lost many, many warriors, their enemies lost far more. Finally the Ashanti reached the coast.

The king of Gyaman, of the Ivory Coast, heard about the wondrous stool and had one made for himself, hoping to gain power, too. This imitation greatly enraged Osai Bonsu, tenth king of the Ashanti. He went to war against the Gyaman, defeated them, and cut off the Gyaman king's head. The gold from the Gyaman stool was melted down, and with it Ashanti goldsmiths made two masks in the defeated king's image. The masks were hung on each side of the golden stool to add more power and wealth to it.

Some enemies of the Ashanti later claimed that their golden stool was really the Gyaman stool that they had captured. The Ashanti only laughed at such rumors.

Each Ashanti's life from childhood to death is bound up with his religion and ceremonies. Most Ashanti do not pray directly to the gods. They are prayed *for* by the chiefs, the queen mothers, the priests and priestesses, the drummers. The people observe the ceremonies by gathering outside their chief's house while the prayers go on inside the stool house.

Not only is the golden stool worshiped, but also the stools on which important chiefs sat. These ancient stools are kept in special rooms, called stool houses, in each chief's household. Every forty-three days the Ashanti observe two days of ceremonies, called Adae, to honor their ancestors, beginning with the worship of their ancestors' stools. These two days, a Sunday and the following Wednesday, are holy days.

The Ashanti divide the week into seven days as we do. But in counting the days of the week, they give each day its turn to head a week. So if Monday is the first day one week, Tuesday will be the first day the following week. Wednesday heads the week after that, Thursday the fourth week, and so on.

| | | | | | | | |
|---|---|---|---|---|---|---|---|
| Monday | Tues | Wed | Thur | Fri | Sat | Sun | 7 days |
| Tuesday | Wed | Thur | Fri | Sat | Sun | Mon | 14 days |
| Wednesday | Thur | Fri | Sat | Sun | Mon | Tues | 21 days |
| Thursday | Fri | Sat | Sun | Mon | Tues | Wed | 28 days |
| Friday | Sat | Sun | Mon | Tues | Wed | Thur | 35 days |
| Saturday | Sun | Mon | Tues | Wed | Thur | Fri | 42 days |
| Sunday—the 43rd day | | | | | | | |

When the first day of the week falls on a Sunday, it is the first day of the Adae ceremony, which honors the sky god as well as the ancestors. Prayers to both take place before altars in the stool houses. There the spirit of the god rests in a special brass tray filled with herbs and other plant materials for the god spirit to use.

The Adae ceremonies occur at the same time among all Ashanti clans, wherever there are stool houses. Not all the stools of the chiefs or the queen mothers are preserved and consecrated. Only the most important are selected to be worshiped.

The stool carriers (an office of honor for both men and women) supervise these Adae ceremonies. After a chief dies and his stool has been found worthy of keeping in a stool house, it is blackened with soot that has been mixed with egg yolk. It is placed on its side, on an elevation, in the back of the stool house. These stools, henceforth, are not moved at all, unless fire threatens the house or war compels a village to move out of range of the enemy. With the passing of the years the wood in these stools begins to rot and finally crumbles into a heap. But the worship of them continues.

The day that precedes the Sunday or Wednesday of the Adae ceremony is spent in preparing for the occasion. The king's stool is scrubbed by his stool carriers. The stool house is aired and its floor swept. The cooks clean all the dishes (usually gourds) that will hold the ceremonial food for the ancestors' stools, and the attendants select a sheep for the sacrifice. Palm wine, rum, and whisky are obtained from the king's storerooms. Also, firewood is piled in the courtyard for broiling the sacrificial sheep. Gold dust, needed for the ceremony, is set aside in a special box.

Captain R. S. Rattray described a Wednesday ceremony he witnessed in the king's stool house. Everyone assembled early. Those who were going to enter the stool house wore their oldest clothes to show humility before their ancestors. The people who participated in the ceremony were the king, the herald and the drummer, the head stool carrier and the other stool carriers, the spokesman, a gun bearer and a sword bearer.

The stools in the dark stool house were covered with a cloth and were ranged against the back wall on a platform about three feet from the ground. As a sign of respect to his ancestors, the king bared his shoulder and stood barefoot on his sandals. Men usually show respect this way when they pray, when they come to greet their king, and when they enter sacred ground. The king's greeting was, "Good morning, spirit grandfathers. Good morning." The stool carrier put his stool behind the king so he could sit down, while the cloth was removed from the ancient stools.

There were three rows of stools, totaling thirteen in all. Some had crumbled with age.

Their edges were caked with the blood and fat of sacrificed sheep. The head stool carrier took a pitcher of fresh water and poured it on the ground, saying, "Grandfather, Eguyayeboaro, receive this water and wash your hands." The cooks brought in a dish of mashed bananas called *eto*. The chief stool carrier took a spoonful and handed it to the king. The king arose, bared his chest, and tucked his toga around his waist. In this humble position he emptied the spoon onto the oldest stool, saying, "My spirit grandfathers, today is the Wednesday Adae. Come receive this *eto* and eat. Let this town prosper. Permit the women to bear healthy children. May all the people who are in this town get riches."

As the king prayed and paused between phrases, his spokesman cried out, "Yo!" The herald chimed in, *"Tie, tie!* (Hear, hear!)"

Only the oldest ancestor was thus addressed by name. The king spooned the *eto* into each of the thirteen stools, saying to each stool, "Grandfather, receive this food and eat." The bowl was then taken out of the stool house and the food was scattered over the ground. In this way the spirits of the stool carriers for the dead chiefs were also fed.

The cooks carried the sheep to be sacrificed into the stool house. They held the struggling animal as the king punctured its neck and the blood spurted into a bowl. Again the king repeated, "Grandfather, Eguyayeboaro, accept this sacrifice of this sheep." The seat and edge of each stool were carefully smeared with the blood. The sacrificed sheep was then carried out.

Outside the meat was being cut up for broiling. Thirteen skewers, one for each stool, were set out. Three pieces of meat were strung on each of the skewers and cooked over the fire. The broiled meat was carried back into the stool house on a large wooden platter. The raw sheep's head was also carried in and put on the ground in front of the stools. A musician rang a bell to announce that the spirits were about to eat. The king placed a skewer of roasted meat on each stool. The cooks added bits of lung to the offering. "Here is meat. Receive it and eat," the king repeated. Each time the herald shouted, "*Tie, tie!*"

The stools were now offered a drink. Whisky was poured into a brass cup. The herald tasted the drink and handed it to the chief stool carrier, who poured a few drops of whisky on each stool. The stool carrier, however, addressed each stool by name, and the spokesman and herald shouted *yo* and *tie* after him.

The rest of the whisky was now poured into the cup. Everyone present took a sip and filed out of the stool house. The king took only one piece of the broiled meat. The rest of the meat was given to the stool carriers and their families.

Outside the crowd waited for the king to come out. But he first went into his house to dress. The drummer began to beat his talking drums, and people listened to them in hushed silence.

The king came out of his house and faced the waiting crowd. His dress was a bright-colored toga made of kente cloth, and it was covered with gold ornaments. His hands and fingers were so full of gold bracelets and rings that he could hardly hold up his arms. On his head he wore a velvet band inlaid with gold. His sandals were decorated with gold figurines. Young boys, bearing ostrich-feather fans and state swords with handles of inlaid gold, followed behind the king. The spokesmen carried gold and silver canes. The treasurer carried an enormous bunch of keys—symbols of many locked storerooms. A sandal bearer carried an extra pair of sandals for the king. Facing the people the king sat down slowly and carefully on his stool. The umbrella carrier shaded him with an immense silk and velvet umbrella.

The talking drums reported to the crowd, "The king has sat down. The destroyer of towns has sat himself down. The powerful one has sat down."

The people, too, seated themselves. Each took his place. Even small children knew where they should sit. Older people had stools their children brought and placed for them. Others sat on the ground.

The ceremony of greeting the king began. One by one subchiefs approached to greet him. Each, as he approached, bared one shoulder and slipped out of his sandals. Each, with a low bow, said, "Grandfather, good morning." Then he turned, slipped back into his sandals, adjusted his toga, and returned to his seat under his own large umbrella.

Attendants with wine cups approached the subchiefs. They took a drink and stood up, in turn, to thank the king.

The Adae ceremony was now over, but the people kept their seat. They were all waiting for the queen mother. She and the women of her household were performing a similar Adae ceremony, honoring the stools of their female ancestors. The women, too, had prayed and sacrificed a sheep in their stool house. When the queen mother, accompanied by several women, arrived, the king handed her a cup of wine. She poured a little of it on the ground with a prayer.

The Sunday Adae ceremony was similar to Wednesday's. Again the stools were honored.

Early on Sunday a woman, carrying a pot of water on her head, stopped at the entrance to the king's compound. She poured the water on the ground, inverted the pot over the wet spot, and placed a stone on the pot. This custom insured the Ashanti against quarreling and strife. Soon after, people began to gather in the streets, while inside the men's and women's stool houses the ceremonies resembling those of Wednesday's Adae were performed.

In forty-two days the ceremonies would be repeated as they have been for hundreds of years.

# 4

## THE FAMILY

The Ashanti believe that a child inherits its father's *ntoro* (en-toh-roh), his soul or spirit. So a child's *ntoro* belongs to his father's clan. But a child's flesh and blood, his *mogya*, come from his mother. He is, therefore, more closely related to his mother's clan, her *abusua*. *Mogya*, blood, and *abusua*, clan, have the same meaning in Ashanti.

The ancestors a person feels closest to are those of his mother. Their spirits will always be at his side to protect him. In turn, he respects them and attends the ceremonies in their honor. There are eight mother clans and nine father clans among the Ashanti. Anthropologists call a mother clan a matrilineal clan and a father clan a patrilineal clan.

To an Ashanti his family and his mother's clan are most important. His loyalty belongs to them first, to the village chief second, and to the king third. When traveling, an Ashanti looks for members of his mother's clan in the village where he wishes to spend the night. He is sure to be received by the villagers like a brother. A clansman's hospitality usually knows no bounds. If he likes the visitor, he may beg him to remain in the village and even to marry his daughter, since she belongs to a different clan.

When a man is expelled from his village because of an offense, the talking drums announce the news. Such a person is no longer considered a clansman even in remote villages. Life for an ousted man can be very lonely, as well as dangerous, since there are no clansmen to care for him and to protect him.

On the other hand, adoption into a clan is done without much public notice. A slave woman who has married an Ashanti man may be accepted along with her children into a father's clan, because they grew up thinking of themselves as members of it. For a while neither she nor her children will be treated as real blood clansmen. But eventually, after a generation or two, their slave origin will be forgotten and their descendants will be considered full-blooded Ashanti.

An Ashanti household is not made up of just a father, mother, and their children, as is our small, close-knit family. It is an extended family, which lives in a large compound. The head of this large household is usually the oldest brother in it. Everyone calls him Father or Housefather, and everyone obeys him.

An Ashanti household consists of many small homes or huts, built around a courtyard. A housefather may have two, three, or more wives. The majority of men, however, have only one wife. Each woman has her own house, where she lives with her children. Her husband also has a house of his own in the center of the compound. There he eats his meals, which his children bring him. Under the floor of this central house an ancestor or two may be buried. Other houses in the compound are occupied by the housefather's younger brothers, married and unmarried nephews, and unmarried sisters.

Married sisters always move to live with their husband's family. There may also be some of the housefather's grandchildren, because his sons married his nieces. In addition, there are slaves and their children.

All these people are wanted, for the household needs many working hands to prosper. The larger the household, the prouder is its housefather. But if a wife feels that her husband makes her work too hard or does not treat

her as well as he treats his other wives, she may
ask her uncle or her brothers to come and take
her home. If the children are small, she will
take them with her. Nevertheless, as the boys
get to be eight and nine years of age, they return to their father to be trained by him in
whatever skills he prefers or in which they show
special liking. Nowadays he also pays for their
schooling, since all children have to attend
school. The father, however, must not teach

them to use talking drums. This skill can only be learned from an uncle—their mother's brother.

Girls remain with their mother, since she has to teach them housekeeping and cooking skills as well as how to grow the important food crops. The fields take up most of a woman's time and energy. She must also bring in food, firewood, and water, so she is busy from dawn to sundown.

A man becomes the head of a household because the elders in it think he is the best one for the difficult job. A man may designate his eldest son, whom he has trained, to succeed him as head of the household. But as a rule an old headman will select his successor for his ability, so that a nephew or his younger brother may be his choice instead.

The post of housefather is an honored one, although it entails many responsibilities. The father has to run a large household successfully and also be custodian of the ancestral spirits, chief administrator of all family property, and judge in family quarrels. No man, however, ever pronounces judgment without first consulting the elders in his household. The elder men and women, in turn, talk things over with the younger people, so that everyone in a household has a voice. No housefather fails to follow family customs, and he expects the other members of the household to act in the same way.

Customs call for respecting personal property. No one has the right to another's tools, ornaments, clothes. No one must violate the clan taboos, such as eating the meat of a totem animal or speaking ancestral names on forbidden days. No one must practice witchcraft, use bad language, or gossip and repeat hearsay. Any offense is considered a crime. Offenders are brought to the headman. Hearings take place in the presence of witnesses, but the final decision is up to the head of the household.

To belong to a household means a great deal to each and every member of such an extended family. It means sharing in both labor and in the fruits and enjoyment of this labor. It means security. No one member of a household ever need stand alone. Whether right or wrong, his family and clan will rally to his aid. They will spend all their resources and even go into debt to help him or her. No person need ever appear alone before a chief to speak for himself. Every member of his family will go with him, ready to vouch for him, whether he is young or old.

A father sets aside property for his sons, since a son does not automatically inherit his father's possessions. Everything a son produces belongs to his father, but his father will present him with sheep and cloth on his birthday. This sheep and its offspring will henceforth belong to the boy. If parents feel that an uncle (mother's brother) has better means and will give their son better opportunities, they may send the boy to him. Should the father die, the son will remain with his uncle, whose property he will eventually inherit. An uncle must never punish his nephew as his own mother and father may. The uncle can do so only with the consent of a boy's parents.

The father may farm a piece of land in his son's name or give his son a kola tree. The land, however, cannot be *given* to the son, for land may *never* be given away or sold to anyone. It belongs to the clan. On his deathbed a father, in the presence of witnesses, may bequeath some of his personal belongings to his son. He cannot will to his son anything he himself inherited from *his* uncle. Nor can he give his son his weapons. They belong to his *abusua*, his blood clan.

Each Ashanti man plays two roles. On one hand he is a father who wishes to give his sons every opportunity to fit them properly for adult life. On the other, he is an uncle and has to be responsible for his sisters' children, his nephews and nieces. These nephews will inherit his property. His nieces may also need some help and supervision. But they will move away to their husband's household after marriage. A man wants his *sumsum* and his ancestors to be left in capable hands, and so he tries to find good wives for his nephews, who remain to care for his household.

There are folktales of mean and cruel uncles, who think only of themselves. A mean uncle has the right, if he finds a rich man willing to marry one of his married nieces, to compel her to divorce her husband. Her children, when they grow up, will come to live with him and bring him the wealth their father gifted to them.

Among the Ashanti childhood and youth are passed in affectionate surroundings. Everyone in the household will offer help to a child and feed him. When he is four or five years old, his hair is cut for the first time. The father has the right to cut off the first lock, and then he presents the child with a sheep and some gold dust. This gift remains the child's property.

Both parents take part in the very early training of an infant. A child is taught never to touch other people's belongings. If he does he is punished. Children learn by imitating their parents and listening to their father and mother at home, at gatherings, at festivals. Parents bring their children to all ceremonies. A son always sits behind his father, and usually he carries his father's stool. A young man never smokes in the presence of his elders. When talking to them, he always removes his headdress. From childhood he has learned to use his right hand for eating and speaking and his left for adjusting his clothes. Both hands are used when receiving a gift. A well-bred Ashanti never stares at a person, unless he is actually speaking to him. People must always wear their best clothes in public.

The Ashanti do not mark with any special ceremonies or initiations their boys' coming of age, as so many other African peoples do. Young men are preoccupied with accumulating the property that they will need to be able to support a wife or, as in some cases, wives. They look forward to being married after they reach the age of twenty-one or twenty-two.

Girls, however, get more attention. A girl's family, her relatives, and friends enjoy a week's celebration when she turns fourteen or fifteen and is on the threshold of adulthood. During this week everyone brings her gifts: gold necklaces, bracelets, silk and cotton cloth for dresses. Her female relatives take her daily to the river for a special bath. Her attendants rub oil all over her body and sprinkle gold dust on her shoulders and arms. They draw bright lines on her face and help her get dressed in her best garments. She then visits friends in the village. Her young attendants accompany her singing her favorite songs. Every hostess greets her joyfully with refreshments, dancing, and singing. Young men will begin to court her now and within a year or two the girl will be married.

The marriage ceremony is simple. The

groom's clan presents a thank-you gift, called *aseda*, to the girl's parents and her clan when they approve the marriage. *Aseda* is not a bride-price. It is rather an agreement to a marriage between two families. Whatever gifts are exchanged, only some are kept by parents of the bride. Half of them go to the bride's uncle. This *aseda* need not be more than a pot of palm wine. A portion of it is poured on the ground in an offering to the ancestors with a simple prayer.

When a woman is about to give birth to a child, she presents her husband with a fowl, which he is to sacrifice to his ancestors while praying for the health of the child. So the child will be born easily, he lets a few drops of blood from the fowl soak into the floor of his wife's hut. He also offers his ancestors *eto*, which his wife has prepared. He then eats a piece of the cooked fowl. So do the wife and their children.

The husband's gift to his pregnant wife is cloth for a white dress and a gold ornament to wear till the child is born. The husband also dresses in white. After eating, they rub white clay on themselves. The husband applies it on the back of his wrists, the wife down the center of her body and around her waist. They also give some *eto* to the earth and sky spirits. The infant is not named till it is eight days old, and the father usually selects the name for his child.

A man is responsible for his wife's debts and for her welfare and the care of their children. But at no time does a man have control over his wife's affairs. Women enjoy great freedom among the Ashanti.

But each Ashanti woman faces the sad fact that her children may leave her and go to live with her brother—their uncle. If her son marries a niece of his father, her grandchildren will be of another clan and will be closer to their grandfather than to her. However, her daughters will remain members of her clan and her daughter's children—her grandchildren—will bear her clan name. But they may not be close by, since her daughters have to live with their husband's clan, as she herself has to live with her husband's people.

A man who inherits his uncle's estate may marry his uncle's wife or wives after a year has elapsed. If a woman does not wish to marry the heir, her family may return the *aseda* given them. But if the woman has children, the children keep the *aseda*. Sometimes when there are no male heirs, the uncle's property goes to his niece. She will then send the wives home to their own clans, but she will not expect the *aseda* to be returned to her.

In the old days many Ashanti families owned slaves. This custom might have arisen out of a still older custom of pawns. Among the Ashanti, as among many other peoples, each family was responsible for debts made by any of its members. When a person could not pay his debts, his family tried to find ways of meeting the obligation. Faced with a crisis, a family might gather for a council to decide how to make an immediate payment against the debt. The person who incurred it might be ill, might be away working in a town, or might have disappeared or died. If the family did not have the necessary gold dust to pay, they sent a younger sister or a brother, provided he or she was acceptable, as a pawn in temporary payment.

The person selected as a pawn could not protest, since custom ruled that he help his family. A pawn knew what was in store for him. Considered his master's property, he worked for him and obeyed him, always hopeful that his own family would be able to raise enough money to repay the debt and thus free him. But sometimes, due to unforeseen circumstances, the person died as a pawn. His family could claim his body, but his children remained in the household of their master as his slaves.

If a female pawn found life in the master's household too hard, she might offer him one of her children, who had grown up, to replace her. If agreeable to the master, this exchange was effected. A woman might also consent to marry the master. Their sons were considered members of the master's clan, and so remained in his household, even after they were married. The daughters, also members of the master's clan, went to live with their husband's people after marriage, but the husband had to buy them.

It may well be that the custom of pawns first took place between related families. The parents did not mind sending their child to work for people in the next house. They could see their child and could make sure that he was treated well. A man or woman given as a pawn could visit his or her family frequently. But as the Ashanti population grew, pawns had to be sent farther away from home. Some pawns were forgotten by their family. Thus the pawn custom may have been the origin of slavery among the Ashanti.

Most slaves, however, were not Ashanti,

whereas a pawn usually was. A slave was purchased by someone who could afford to pay the price. His master could sell him without notifying anyone. When added to the household, he was expected to do the menial jobs that an Ashanti (man or woman) wished to avoid. Slaves were easily recognized, whether at home or in public. Their clothing was of the poorest at all times, and they were not permitted to wear gold ornaments. Usually a slave wore a metal or stone armband on his right arm and a tribal tattoo on his face and body. Ashanti do not like to tattoo themselves. A tattooed person, even if he belongs to a royal clan, cannot become a chief.

The main slave market was at Salaga in the Northern Territories. The Ashanti recall that the Salaga market used to be a place for all sorts of trade goods, cattle, and sheep as well as for slaves. The groups of slaves were shackled with irons on their legs and tied by ropes so they could not slip away and vanish into the forest. An Ashanti usually sold his supply of kola nuts and received cowrie shells or gold dust in payment. With his bags of cowrie shells the man then went to the marketplace to inspect the slaves. He decided whether he wanted to buy a woman or a man. A woman was worth almost twice the price, because she was expected to bear children, which would belong to the master. The master did not have to pay in full for the slave. He could leave a deposit of cowrie shells and take the slave home with him to see how well he worked and whether he was worth the price.

A runaway slave, if caught outside Ashanti land limits, could be killed by his master. But if caught within the Ashanti lands, the master had to take the slave to his chief. There both the master and the slave got a hearing to see whether the slave's escape was justifiable. If the slave deserved killing, the chief's executioner did the job. With wartime and abundance of captives, the Ashanti began to honor their stools by sacrificing slaves to them. However, no slave could be sacrificed unless the chief approved.

Defeated chiefs sent warriors to the victors

as tribute. These men began as pawns in their own lands and ended up as slaves to the Ashanti. Still they kept their hopes that they would one day be redeemed by their family. A man who committed a crime and was, therefore, disowned by his clan could become a voluntary slave in a household far away from his own village. In this way he found a place to belong, where he could live and work.

On the whole the Ashanti treated their slaves with consideration. There were instances when a trusted slave, having joined his master's clan, later became the master's sole heir. A master was responsible for his slave's acts. If the slave committed a crime, the master had to supply compensation. Some slaves who were skilled craftsmen became rich enough to purchase a slave to work for them. Among the Ashanti a slave might marry either a slave woman or a free woman. A free woman's children belonged to her clan, so if a slave wanted his children to remain with him he preferred to marry a slave woman in his master's household.

Slaves had separate burial grounds, since

usually no ceremonial funeral was held for them. However, the master of a beloved slave might sacrifice a fowl and fast for a day. The sacrifice and fasting would help the slave find his place among his dead ancestors.

# 5

## THE GOVERNMENT

The Ashanti arranged their government and their way of living in the form of a pyramid, and their system was all the more remarkable because it had been worked out by a nonliterate people.

The king's household fitted into the top of the pyramid. At the base were the villages, scattered all over the lands of the Ashanti. Each village was made up of many large households, each with its housefather. Each village also had a village head. The village head's council was made up of heads of households. The villages were united under a subchief. The subchiefs, in turn, sat on a District Council of Elders. A district chief presided over the council, and the district chiefs were united under a paramount chief. There were fifteen such paramount chiefs. They made up the Ashanti Confederacy Council, which was headed by the king and which met at Kumasi.

Originally the Ashanti lived in tribal settlements made up of many clans. Each such settlement was independent of all the rest. It lived by hunting, fishing, farming, and trading, and it regarded its lands as belonging exclusively to it. No outsider was permitted to farm, hunt, fish, or cross these tribal lands unless he paid a fee or received special permission. Even in the old days the king hardly interfered in regional affairs. They were left entirely to the regional chiefs.

When people of two villages could not settle in councils disputed boundary rights or fishing rights, they did not go to war. Instead, they selected two men, one from each village, to fight each other with their swords. Everyone gathered to see the combat, which in itself helped to dissolve some of the bitterness and tension of the quarrel. Obviously each village sided with its champion and prayed for him. Villagers brought with them all the charms they owned to assure victory. But at the same time the people of both villages met and mingled and talked. Wielding their shields, the two men fought till they were fatigued. It was not necessary for one opponent to kill the other. Whoever came out victor, because of his finer swordsmanship, was considered to have won the argument for his village. And soon the quarrel was forgotten.

Settlements grew in size as the population grew. When a village became too crowded, families wandered off to found new settlements. Such new settlements became important cities: Kokofu, Juaben, and Kumasi. Originally Kumasi was called Kwaman. Legend has it that Okomfo Anokye planted two seedlings of the *kum* tree—one at Kwaman, the other at another town. The second seedling died; the first, at Kwaman, thrived. This sign was the supernatural one that Anokye expected. Therefore, he renamed the town Kumasi in honor of the seedling and designated it as the capital of the Ashanti.

In cases where the forests, fields, and rivers no longer yielded a livelihood, the people packed their belongings and moved to a fresh area. There they set about clearing and burning the forest land for farms. Thus the city of Mampong was settled by the Ashanti tribes called Adanse, Nsuta, and Kumaw.

In time the Ashanti, due to pressure of coastal tribes, were forced back northward from where they had originally come. These southern coastal groups had been trading with the Europeans. From them they acquired guns and ammunition and began to use them against their neighbors. But toward the end of the seventeenth century the Ashanti also acquired guns in trade with the Europeans and they, in turn, began warring against neighboring tribes.

The pomp and splendor of the coastal courts must have aroused the Ashanti chiefs' wish for the same. Okomfo Anokye and Osai Tutu were convinced that the Ashanti could be equally great, but that they needed to unite first. To unite into a single confederacy and to acknowledge one man, Osai Tutu, as head was a big departure from the customary independence of the Ashanti chiefs. But Osai Tutu and Okomfo

Anokye must have been very persuasive. The regional chiefs agreed to unite, and the Ashanti nation was thus launched into a Confederacy and into greatness.

Osai Tutu was elected overall chief, or king. In Ashanti the word for king is *hene* (pronounced hay-nay). *Omanhene* means tribal chief; *oman* means tribe. Osai Tutu was thenceforth called *Asantehene*—king of the Ashanti. Kumasi, where Osai Tutu had been a tribal chief, an *omanhene*, now became the capital of the Ashanti confederacy. All chiefs and sub-chiefs readily swore their loyalty oath. Among the Ashanti such an oath could not be broken without risking death.

In addition to being crowned *Asantehene*, Osai Tutu was also given ownership of all Ashanti lands. The Ashanti lands belonged to clans. Each family head, representing his clan, had the right to tell his people which piece of land they could cultivate. Osai Tutu was now granted a voice in making these decisions. If a person felt he was unjustly treated in a piece of land selected for him, he could carry his grievance not only to his own regional chief, but to the *Asantehene* himself.

In return for the power granted him, Osai Tutu assigned honorary stools to the fifteen confederacy chiefs. Sharing stools with the *Asantehene* meant the chiefs were very close to Osai Tutu; they were his brothers. This arrangement also assured Osai Tutu that he would have all the chiefs on his side, since brothers do not fight among themselves.

The title of *hene* was also given to the Ashanti elders, who became advisers to Osai Tutu and his court. These elders were accustomed to advise their own village housefathers, and they readily took on the new advisory duties. Osai Tutu, in addition, made them into commanders of the Ashanti army in wartime.

Osai Tutu's mother was also his adviser. Since descent among the Ashanti is counted through the mother's clan, the head of the royal clan is the queen mother. Osai Tutu's mother, therefore, became queen mother. She attended all councils, sitting on her son's left. Her advice depended on what the older women and men with whom she had talked counseled her. A queen mother did not have to be the mother or sister of the chief, though. She could be his grandmother or his aunt. When a chief died or lost his stool, he might be replaced by his brother or by an uncle or nephew. All these men belonged to the royal clan, and the queen mother was their head. So she retained her title.

Since the survival of a clan depended on its women, there was fear that the Ashanti might lose a clan due to the death of girl infants or mothers. In wartime the chief's wives went to war with him, since they were not members of the royal clan, but his mother and his sisters could not go. The Ashanti feared that if their clan died out, their ancestors would remain in the cold, shadowless spirit world with no one left on earth to pay honor to them. In the past, when a clan was so threatened, men went about neighboring villages looking for young women who belonged to their clan. When they found them, they took them back to their own village, gave them the best of care and attention, and begged them to marry men of the village. Their children would be an assurance for themselves and for their ancestors that the clan would continue.

The ceremony of crowning an *Asantehene*, or, as the Ashanti say, *enstooling* the *Asantehene*, was elaborate only in the large gathering of the people, their festive dress, the music, the gun firing, and the talking drums. Everyone assembled in the town square before the chief's house. The *Asantehene* appeared in his dazzling dress. Attendants brought out the golden stool and, supporting their chief, let him bend his knees three times into a sitting position next to the stool. He never sat on it.

The herald announced to the *Asantehene* what was expected of him:

We do not wish that he should disclose the origin of any person.
He must never abuse anyone.
He must never use personal violence.
He must not call people fools.
He must not be greedy.
His ears should never be hard of hearing (meaning he should willingly listen to everyone).
He should never say I have no time to hear you.
He should never act without consulting others.

To this speech the *Asantehene* replied, "If I do not rule the people well, as my forefathers and you ruled them, and if I do not listen to advice of the councilors, then I have broken my oath and may be punished." The punishment was beheading.

A chief (any chief—not only the *Asantehene*) was held in great respect by all the people because of the sacred stool he occupied. In every Ashanti's opinion a chief spoke not only his own mind but that of his ancestors. He prayed and kept his ancestors advised of his decisions. A good chief asked his elders for advice and saw to it that the village heads managed their own affairs well. It was important that everyone keep up with his responsibilities. They must not lean too much on the *Asantehene* in governing their people.

Old age and illness might force the council to destool a chief, whether he was the *Asantehene* or a regional chief. This act, however, could be done only with the consent of the queen mother and of the other women in the royal clan. To keep the peace, the destooled chief was asked to leave with only one wife and a servant and a little gold dust. He had to live in a village far removed from the center of government, and he must never return to the town. Should he return, he might be put to death.

To run the chief's big household called for great expenditures of money. In the old days money was sent to the chief in the form of gold dust. A measure called a *pereguan* was an amount of gold worth about twenty-five dollars. This *pereguan* was divided into smaller bundles of gold dust with which the treasurer paid various obligations incurred in the chief's household. While working there a craftsman received his food and lodging. When he left, the treasurer paid him in gold dust for whatever he produced. He might have tooled leather or tanned it. He might have been a weaver or a goldsmith, an ivory tusk carver or a sculptor in wood, a maker of swords or of bows and arrows. Even though he could neither read nor write, the craftsman kept a careful mental record of what he produced. When it came time to settle for the work done, he stated the exact sum due him. There were no disputes.

The gold dust was kept in the safety of the chief's sleeping chamber. He could watch his treasure and so could the spirits of the ancestors. Not many would dare to steal in their presence. Three or four men, rather than one, always handled the incoming and outgoing funds. The same number witnessed each exchange of trade goods and gold. In this way the people's memory was aided, and individuals also checked up on one another.

The dividing of income within the chief's household was set up by law and custom. No one received very large sums, but each sum that came into the treasury from tribute was dribbled out to various people. When a man died, for example, his family had to pay the chief for the loss of a subject. While trading, each merchant paid a fee according to size for the loads that his carriers brought to market to sell. Throughout the lands of the Ashanti traders had to pass barriers, leading from one territory to another. At the borders stood guards collecting fees from these merchants. On their return journey, with merchandise purchased after selling their own goods, the merchants again had to pay a fee to leave the territory.

There were also court fines and fees. They were paid to a chief to thank him for his judgment, and the Ashanti called them along with gifts for the chief *aseda*. *Aseda* was divided among the chief, the queen mother, and all other people who had to attend court during a trial.

When a man committed an offense, his kinsmen could save his life by paying a sum called realistically blood money. Since only a chief could pardon a criminal, the case had to be carried to him and the money was paid to him, too.

Another tax was levied on mines. A clan received one third of the income from a gold mine on their lands. The remainder went to the chief. The chiefs, in turn, paid out monies to the *Asantehene* for the upkeep of his household.

From the beginning of the eighteenth century to the beginning of the twentieth century, the Ashanti warred and claimed ownership of the lands they conquered. The chiefs' treasuries were filled with tribute from the subdued peoples. In between wars each chief ruled his own domain and was independent. In wartime, because of his oath, he obeyed the *Asantehene*, his commander in chief.

Although the Ashanti were considered the bravest fighters of West Africa, their army was made up mostly of slaves and conquered people. Theirs was guerrilla fighting. Men kept out of sight of their enemy and sniped at him unexpectedly. In the first rank of fighters were the scouts. They were mainly hunters from the north, who used long sticks. With the sticks they shook the trees to trick the enemy into firing and revealing his location. Although the scouts also carried guns, they did not shoot at the beginning of a battle. It was considered unlucky for a scout to be killed, so they avoided direct fire. As soon as they had revealed the enemy, they retired to the rear and were replaced by the line behind them. In this manner line after line advanced to fire at the enemy, while the rear lines reloaded and readied themselves for their next turn.

Sword-bearers came behind the advance guard lines. These men carried whips, as well as swords, to flog anyone who attempted to flee from battle.

The regular army followed the advance guard. The chiefs remained in the rear with their bodyguard, and the rear guard was posted behind the chiefs. When the enemy turned to flight, the rear guard chased him. Each army unit had its leader, a chief who was called the pusher. The leader urged his men to battle.

The chiefs' positions were safe as long as the Ashanti warriors held their ground. In case of defeat, however, the soldiers might scatter. The chiefs and commanders then surrounded the golden stool, which was always carried into battle because of its supernatural power. Chiefs were ready to pay for the safety of the stool with their lives. Rather than let the enemy take possession of it, the chiefs and their retainers would burn the stool and themselves with it. If forced to choose between death and loss of the stool, the chiefs would have chosen death.

The army was self-supporting. In addition to his sword, his gun, large shield and stick, a warrior also carried a skin bag of dried bananas, cassava, beans, flour, and ground peppers. If a warrior had a slave, the slave carried everything except the gun. A younger brother who accompanied a warrior carried provisions for both. Younger brothers thus learned warfare. The horn blowers, the flutists, and drummers, in addition to carrying their own gear, also carried some of the chief's food and stayed close to their chief.

After a time away from home, the soldiers tried to live off the country they invaded. This attempt was not always satisfactory, so that everyone hoped the war would last for only a few battles.

There was no sanitation. A medicine man went with the army to help the wounded with potions. Wives of the greater chiefs sometimes accompanied their husband. Some women were in charge of a blackened ancestral stool and carried it. Brave women carried water to the firing line.

The talking drums that accompanied the chiefs were also used as morale builders, in addition to giving the soldiers the news of home and praising their captains' bravery. The talking drums were always generous with praise of great deeds, but they did not speak of defeats. Ashanti, as a rule, do not like to talk of defeats and bad times. They do not even like to admit that an important man was killed in battle. Instead, the drummers proclaimed that a chief disappeared—like a rock that sinks into a lake. When an ancestor's stool was burned in defeat, the drummers told the people that the elders and the stool disappeared with the chief.

A man who showed cowardice in battle was killed, unless his family was able to buy his life from the chief with a payment of gold dust. However, even though his life was spared, the man had to wear woman's beads around his waist, his eyebrows were shaved, and his hair was combed in a special way that marked him to everyone as a coward.

Enemy soldiers captured in these wars were turned into slaves. Since their villages were often destroyed and their family and kin scat-

tered, there was no one to buy the conquered warriors' freedom. These captives became either slaves in a chief's household or were given away as gifts to brave warriors or sold to Ashanti traders. They were then brought to the coastal towns to be shipped to the West Indies and the Americas. Some who remained in Africa were able to marry and eventually became members of their master's household. Their children bore the clan name of their master and regarded themselves as Ashanti.

# 6 THE ASHANTI AND THE EUROPEANS

The first Europeans to reach the Gulf of Guinea on the coast of West Africa were the Portuguese in 1471. They found that the people had gold to sell and plunged into trading that gained enormous profits for them. Some ten years later, in 1481, the Portuguese built their first castle on the coast. They called it Elmina (the mine, meaning the gold mine). In reality, the castle was a fort, intended to safeguard the Portuguese themselves, their goods, and the gold they received in trade. Later Elmina also held the imprisoned Africans who were to be sold into slavery to Europeans and Americans.

During the first three centuries of trade with West Africa, the Europeans were kept in fear and ignorance of the rich interior. They did not even feel safe along the coast. The names of the peoples with whom they were trading

were unknown, and all Africans were called Akan. The Akan made it clear to the Portuguese from the start that they were not on their own soil. Their trading was welcome, but they must take gifts to the chiefs in order to continue trading and building castles. The Portuguese had no choice but to accept these terms, since the Akan were too numerous to fight. As trade expanded, the Portuguese built another fort along the coast at Axim in 1503.

Despite this insecure existence, the Portuguese continued their profitable trading. With threats they kept the African villages around them from attacking the forts. If any African destroyed Portuguese property, or if an African trader failed to pay a debt, the Portuguese garrison sallied forth, fully armed. The first villagers they met were caught and imprisoned, regardless of guilt. These innocent people were released only after the debt was paid. Bad feeling and resentment, first of the Portuguese and later of all European traders, were thus built up.

Some fifty years after the arrival of the Portuguese, the English began to establish themselves on the coast of West Africa despite Portuguese threats. Englishmen were received with as much suspicion as the Portuguese. So the English, who had fought with the Portuguese in European waters, faced a double threat: unfriendly and suspicious Africans and hostile Portuguese, who never hesitated to destroy their competitors.

In the seventeenth century several other European powers began trading in the Gulf of

Guinea for gold, and the region became known as the Gold Coast. In 1602 a Dutch trader described trading there. He wrote that African traders brought their loaded carriers from the interior to the coast. These merchants had already crossed many tribal lands, where they had to pay tribute for permission to pass through. On the coast they had to pay tribute again for permission to sell their goods to the Europeans. After purchasing European trade goods, the merchants paid a fee to leave the coast. As they progressed into the interior, they paid fees for permission to return to their countries with the trade goods. These merchants also bought slaves on the coast to carry loads back inland.

Loading and unloading ships was a most dramatic and dangerous venture on the Gulf of Guinea coast. The steep, uneven coastline, with its overhanging cliffs, provided no secure harbor. So European ships had to anchor far offshore, depending on the skilled African canoemen to bring passengers and their goods safely ashore. Coming and going the large canoes made use of wind and tides. Goods and passengers were dropped from the ship into waiting canoes. Loaded, the canoes maneuvered skillfully over great waves, rollers, and breakers to shore. The steep rollers lifted the canoes dangerously high, threatening men and cargo with spilling. And sometimes they did spill. As a roller receded, the Africans paddled furiously, making the boat leap forward to avoid the foaming breakers that followed the rollers. The canoe shot forward, timed by the paddlers to land high on the beach with the spent breaker. There more men waited to lift passengers and cargo onto safe ground.

African traders, carrying little pouches and boxes of gold dust, often came in canoes directly to the anchored ships. There the Europeans placed their trade goods on display. The Africans examined them carefully and selected what they wanted. This careful inspection of European goods became necessary, since the Africans often found that in a pack of brass basins the Europeans might insert some broken and damaged ones that would prove useless. They might also slip rotten and inferior material into bolts of cloth. If the Europeans agreed to the amount of gold that the African traders offered, deals were concluded and the cargo removed into the canoes. If the Africans could not agree on the price or if they did not like the quality of the trade goods, they left. The following day they might return for further inspection and bargaining. Trading directly aboard ship freed the owners from having to face the ever-watchful Portuguese officials.

The proud Ashanti people so shunned outsiders that Europeans knew practically nothing about their way of life. Goods supplied by the Ashanti chiefs were brought to the Gold Coast by African traders of other tribes and there sold to Europeans. The same African traders then carried European trade goods back inland to the Ashanti. The interior, unknown to the Europeans, was well governed, organized, and guarded so traders could travel in safety, even if they had to pay tribute. It is interesting to note the large quantities of trade goods that were absorbed by these people of the interior. They were rich enough to pay for luxuries and ready to accept foreign goods, although they wanted goods of high quality only.

The trade goods the Ashanti received consisted of cotton, silk, and woolen goods, hatchets and knives, beads, iron, lead, tobacco, tobacco pipes, guns, gunpowder, and brass vessels. These brass vessels were in great demand all over West Africa. They were so durable that they replaced the perishable gourds and earthen pots the people had been using. The goods the Ashanti traded were gold, elephants' tusks, skins, timber, wax, palm oil, and slaves. The number of slaves sold increased as the demand for them grew in the developing countries of the West Indies and the Americas.

In 1621 the Dutch traders entered fully into competition for this trade. The powerful Dutch West India Company built a fort at Mori, in 1624. Their trade goods were lower priced and outsold those of the Portuguese. The Portuguese, in the meantime, developed other trading interests farther east and south along the African coast and began to move away. Elmina and Axim were taken over by the Dutch.

Competition among the European countries increased when the Swedes arrived in 1645 and the Danes in 1657. These traders, too, wanted to buy slaves.

The English did not hesitate to side with one group of Africans against another. These tribes were grateful for help given them and promised to deal exclusively with the British, paying them taxes on goods bought and sold. In this way small British protectorates were established on the Gold Coast. The English built forts at Kormatin and Sekondi, and ousted the Dutch from a castle they had built at Cape Coast.

In 1694, for example, the coastal Akan tribes revolted against their middlemen traders and invited the English at Cape Coast to help them. The Dutch at Elmina agreed to help the enemy tribes against the British. When the British emerged victorious, the Akan chiefs swore allegiance to them.

Traffic in slaves and gold helped the Ashanti rise to power. Around 1700 they began to receive firearms in trade from Europeans, and

they used these arms to overcome their neighboring tribes. The Ashanti had warred before
the coming of the Europeans, but the battles
had been small-scale guerrilla raids, fought
with bows and arrows, and swords. With firearms they were able to subject an enemy com-
pletely. Some of the defeated warriors were sent
to the coast to be sold as slaves. Others were
made to fight with the Ashanti against their
enemies. In time the Ashanti conquered most of
the Gold Coast and became the mightiest nation
in West Africa.

From the fifteenth century to the middle of
the nineteenth the importance of the slave trade
equalled that of the gold trade. An estimated
twenty to thirty million slaves were taken out
of Africa during these four and a half centuries. The Ashanti did not, of course, have
their hand in *all* this slave traffic, but they were
the chief suppliers of slaves for the Gold Coast
trade. And their wealth grew.

In 1802 the Danes ended their slave trade.
The British followed in 1807 and proceeded to
prevent all other powers from crossing the At-

lantic with slave ships. They were largely un-
successful, although traffic in slaves did slow
down. In the Americas by this time the domes-
tic slave population was growing fast enough
to keep up with the demand, so fewer and fewer
slaves had to be imported.

The string of European forts that lined the
Gold Coast became useless, for they were no
longer needed as prisons to hold captives till
they were loaded onto slave ships. The European powers tried to sell them at bargain prices
to each other. What were they to do with these
forts? England's answer was to use them as
trade centers for palm oil, timber, gold, and
diamonds. A peaceful trade thus sprang up. It
proved profitable for the coastal people and undoubtedly even more profitable for the British.

The Ashanti chiefs were puzzled by these
changes. They could not understand why it had
been right to buy and sell slaves for three hundred years and suddenly had become wrong.
The Ashanti never felt any guilt about slave
traffic. The slaves were war captives, and so the

Ashanti had every right to dispose of them. The slaves that they bought at Salaga for re-sale were to them trade goods—to buy and sell.

The Ashanti conquests continued, since their confederacy depended on this way of life. They may also have been afraid that once they dismissed their warriors, the defeated tribes would revolt. The Ashanti would then lose all the territory that they had gained in centuries of fighting. They may have felt that they owed it to the *sumsums* of their ancestors, killed in battles, to retain their lands. So in 1807 the Ashanti, in their advance toward the coast, laid siege to the English fort at Anomabu.

The English were not strong enough at that time to fight the Ashanti alone. Their representatives negotiated with the *Asantehene* at Kumasi and agreed on peaceful trading. However, some twenty years later, the British decided to fight the Ashanti. They promised the coastal tribes to help them in a revolt against the Ashanti conquerors. In 1826 the Ashanti met the coastal tribes in a battle at the town of

Dodowa, and the English supplied rockets for their allies. The balls of fire and explosions struck at the Ashanti without warning, and they suffered a crushing defeat. The coastal tribes unanimously acknowledged the British as their protectors. Thus the entire Gold Coast became a British protectorate, extending from the Gulf of Guinea to the lands of the Ashanti.

Opinion began to be expressed in newspapers and churches throughout the world that nothing was being done to help Africans improve their living standards and to educate them. So the British permitted missions and churches to become established along the Gold Coast.

In 1839 the Reverend T. B. Freeman came to Kumasi and persuaded the *Asantehene* to permit the building of a Christian mission and church at Kumasi. He later presented the *Asantehene* with the first wheeled carriage the Ashanti had ever seen, since they had not as yet domesticated draft animals. Reverend Freeman was permitted to stay in Kumasi, but he was not very successful in gaining converts.

By this time some of the wealthy Africans on

the Gold Coast had begun to send their children to Europe to be educated. Life in West Africa was becoming more and more bearable to Europeans. True, they were still some decades removed from air-conditioned homes, offices, and hotels, but quinine had been discovered as a preventive for malaria, which plagued the coast. Europeans began to feel more hopeful about survival. They could bring their families with them and stay longer.

White children were born and grew up on the Gold Coast. However, they were still called Europeans, although some had never seen Europe. On the other hand, the Negroes were called Africans, even if an African was born during his parents' stay in Europe. The names referred to color rather than national origin.

In 1872 the Dutch sold their last possessions to the British, so the entire coastline was under British influence. The Ashanti, however, immediately claimed that the fort of Elmina belonged to them. To meet this challenge the British decided, in 1874, to move into the interior, on the wide road that had been built from the coast to Kumasi, and to attack the capital. Preparations for this war were announced in the European papers and young men, eager to gain fame, rushed to enlist.

News of this campaign also appeared in the United States, and the *New York Herald* sent its roving reporter, Henry M. Stanley, to cover the war. Stanley wrote some vivid accounts for his American readers. However, since he was not able to get to Kumasi, he had to gather the news secondhand. Actually no reporter ever saw the Ashanti fight. Ashanti guerrillas, as usual, hid in the bush and hills and sniped at the British troops. They were seldom seen. Finally the British reached Kumasi. Although it was a ruined and deserted town when their troops arrived, they burned it anyway.

Since the Ashanti no longer stood guard over the borders of the Northern Territories, the British set out to explore this land, hoping to arrange for commercial ties. They reached Salaga, but found it was no longer a booming market. The Ashanti had stopped buying slaves and selling kola nuts. Trading in cattle had also declined.

The British turned back. In 1876 they moved headquarters from Cape Coast to Accra to keep better control over trade, which was now expanding toward the eastern half of the Gold Coast. There was much smuggling to avoid paying the British taxes on trade goods coming inland from the coast.

The Ashanti losses were so great that they did not rebuild their ruined towns. Years after the British invasion the towns still bore the scars of fighting. Kumasi's wide streets were overgrown with grass. Buildings were neglected. The pomp and splendor were gone. But the Ashanti were still a nation. They still observed their religious ceremonies. They were still independent and prosperous, and they still mined gold. Kintampo became an important trading center in place of Salaga.

In 1895 and 1896 the British sent another force into Ashanti territory. The troops built a fort in Kumasi and ordered the Ashanti to stop their wars, so there would be uninterrupted, peaceful trade. King Prempeh, who was the sixteenth king of the Ashanti, gave in to the British without the expected rebellion and fighting, voluntarily going into exile. This behavior surprised those who knew the Ashanti as brave warriors. Years after the reason why they did not fight was learned. The British, the Ashanti believed, would have been sure to win, since they had superior arms. In such an important war the Ashanti would have had to take their golden stool to battle. Rather than lose the golden stool, the *Asantehene* and his councilors decided to let the lands of the Ashanti become a British protectorate. Later the British let King Prempeh return from exile.

For the next five years peace reigned between the two powers. But in March of 1900 a British governor, visiting Kumasi, inquired about the golden stool. He said he was disappointed to find that on an important occasion such as his visit, the Ashanti did not bring out the golden stool so he might sit on it in honor of his queen. At that time Queen Victoria was still on the British throne.

The assembled Ashanti were shocked by this demand. No one had ever sat on the golden stool. When the stool was still new in their possession, Okomfo Anokye had made an albino African sit down on it. As the albino touched the stool, he disappeared into it. Anokye then ordered that no albino or any European, who was white like an albino, should ever touch the stool. Enraged by the British demands, the Ashanti chiefs hid the golden stool and declared war.

It took a year of fighting and bloodshed to subdue the Ashanti, and in the end their lands were declared a colony of the British Crown. Soon after the British declared the Northern Territories a Northern Territory Protectorate of England. German and French powers laid claims to other sections of West Africa, and the British were thus able to secure their holdings.

For the next twenty-one years nothing was heard of the golden stool. By that time only the old people knew of its hiding place. In 1921 workmen, digging a new government road, struck with their shovels the two great brass pans in which the stool had been hidden and buried. Ashanti elders arrived just in time to prevent the stool from being dug up. They scared off the workmen by telling them that the *sumsum* of smallpox, which the Africans so fear, was buried there and would attack anyone who touched the spot. That night seven elders dug up the stool and hid it in a chief's stool house.

News of the find spread. Some reckless young Ashanti, to whom the golden stool did not hold the same sacred meaning, stripped off some of its gold ornaments and brought them to the market to sell. Fortunately, an old woman recognized the gold as belonging to the stool. She sounded the alarm. The thieves were caught and would have been beheaded right there in the marketplace if the British police had not grabbed them and locked them in the safety of the town jail.

Over the years the golden stool has earned the respect of outsiders since it means so much to the Ashanti, and further unpleasant incidents have been avoided. At present the golden stool is safe with the Ashanti nation.

# 7

## GOLD
## AND
## CRAFTS

The Gold Coast was favored with good soils, timber, and minerals. Among the mineral resources gold was particularly important.

How long and how much gold had been mined before the coming of the Portuguese is not known, since no written records were kept then nor were the exports organized under any one government. But the gold trade must have been going on for a long time in the interior. One indication is that when the Portuguese first asked for gold in trade, they were offered gold ornaments rather than gold dust. Evidently the Gold Coast craftsmen—the Ashanti among them—had already perfected great skill in goldsmithing by that time.

Gold was soft enough for a craftsman to handle easily, and he could mold or hammer out designs of lasting beauty in it. In the days before the Europeans arrived, therefore, gold was prized for ornaments that could be made from it. Sometimes it was used as currency, although in general cowrie shells served as money for West Africans.

The easiest way to obtain gold was by panning the soil and sand from riverbeds, where waters that had flowed over gold-bearing rocks deposited their sediments. After a heavy rain men and women with bowls and basins assembled at the seashore, riverbanks, and streams to pan gold.

A man scooped up a bowl of sand and water and twirled it round and round, washing the contents over the rim. Since the gold grains and flakes were heavier than sand, they sank to the bottom as the sand was washed away. He continued twirling each bowlful till only a spoonful of the sand remained. This residue he took home. There he finished washing out all the sand.

Sometimes, after a day's labor, a man found no gold at all. Sometimes he found only a few flakes. A few times, but not very often, he found gold nuggets. However, since gold panning called for no special skills or tools, many people were willing to devote time to it, always hoping for a big find.

By tracing the source of river waters that carried gold, the people must have come upon the quartz veins and other rocks that held it. Lacking tools for excavating and crushing the rock, however, the Ashanti worked these gold-bearing rocks only to a very limited extent. They found that dealing in slaves was easier than mining for gold. Later, when gold became important in trade with Europeans, the Ashanti put their slaves to work in mines.

The slaves, each in an appointed spot, dug long galleries and shafts. It is reported that nine slaves might work in nine pits in a small area of twelve square yards. Pans were lowered to the slave for the rock that he dug up. Above ground other slaves, under their master's watchful eye, crushed the rock and panned the gold.

In the old days a slave remained at his post, digging down and down, till he reached water or till the vein was exhausted. Since water was not pumped out from the mines in those days, the slave was hoisted up on reaching water level. All this time he stayed at his post, sleeping and eating there. Food and water were lowered down to him.

After the Portuguese landed, they mined gold-bearing ores at Elmina for a time. The Africans never willingly entered the mines. When one of the tunnels collapsed and buried the miners, the Africans were sure that the collapse was due to an angry god who objected to the foreigners digging deep into the earth. In 1636 an earthquake led to another cave-in and loss of lives in a mine at Aowin, which the Portuguese were working. This accident was further proof to the Africans that the gods were against this type of mining.

The Ashanti, with great foresight, kept the source of their gold a secret. They did not want the Europeans to take it over. So until 1877 the mines at Tarkwa, Obuasi, Konog, and Bibiani remained in Ashanti hands.

In those days the gold from the mines was handled by the subchiefs. The subchiefs paid the *Asantehene* a share out of the gold collected.

The chiefs and the *Asantehene* turned over some of their gold to traders, who carried it to the coastal areas and exchanged it for European articles. Each chief specified to the merchant what he needed and the merchant brought the goods back. The goods were then divided and subdivided among the villages, to whom the land belonged by inheritance. Each chief turned the surplus gold over to his court goldsmith, who fashioned artistic articles and jewelry for him and his household. The chief, his family, and retainers wore and carried these articles during ceremonials for the people to view and admire.

In 1877 the rich, gold-bearing quartz veins were opened to Europeans. The man who succeeded in changing the minds of the Ashanti was a Frenchman named Pierre Bonnat. He had been a prisoner of the Ashanti and so got to know their country well. Bonnat estimated that the Ashanti gold industry had been flourishing for at least fifty years before he acquired several of the mines.

Bonnat acted as promoter and soon sold the

mines to European companies. By 1882 six European mining companies were established in the Tarkwa-Aboso area. But mining operations did not begin due to lack of roads and railroads. Legends of Ashanti gold attracted prospectors from all over Europe. As is true of most gold rushes, very few of the get-rich-quick schemes were ever fulfilled. There was no way to transport the heavy machinery needed for profitable gold mining, so the small prospectors came and left.

Eventually, the companies arranged to have their heavy machinery dismantled when it reached the Gold Coast ports. From there it was carried inland on the backs of slaves. A slave could walk about fifteen miles a day and carry a load of between sixty and one hundred pounds. Finally mine owners succeeded in getting a road built from Sekondi to Tarkwa, and between 1901 and 1912 several lines of rails were laid that extended as far as Tarkwa, Obuasi, and Prestea. Gold panning was also mechanized. Dredges were brought in which could scoop up sand that settled in rivers after rains. This sand was washed mechanically through a series of large tanks instead of by the slow hand operations.

The Ashanti were still reluctant to work in mines. But with the opening up of the Northern Territories, its people came to work. Geologists in the meantime were studying the gold deposits and their research brought about more efficient mining methods. Mines were dug deeper; tunnels with ample supports were safer. Air was pumped into the hot interior and water pumped out.

The gold that came from the Gold Coast was of such superior quality that it commanded more money per ounce on the world market than any other. The whole area of West Africa that borders on the Gulf of Guinea was known also as the Guinea Coast. So the British labeled the gold from the Gold Coast as guinea gold. The English pound was made up of twenty shillings, but when the pound was backed by guinea gold, it was valued at twenty-one shillings. So when the British quoted a price of one guinea for an article, they meant twenty-one instead of twenty shillings. To this day the British still use the term guinea.

For some five hundred years, beginning with the arrival of the Portuguese, gold was exported from the Gold Coast. It is estimated that from 1478 to 1903 some sixty-five million dollars' worth of gold was traded. Since then, with mining machinery and railroads, the average annual export of gold has been valued at thirty million dollars. This trade still continues, and today gold is the third ranking export of Ghana.

Some of the goldwork of the Ashanti goldsmiths is now on display at the Smithsonian National Museum in Washington. There are also rich exhibits at the British Museum in London as well as at museums in Ghana. At the Smithsonian the exhibits are mainly artistic gold weights. These weights were owned by individual Ashanti chiefs and merchants, who used them in weighing gold that they traded among themselves or sold to Europeans. Although the weights were not standardized, traders dealing with one another came to know the ones each used. Nephews inherited them from an uncle, and they were a valuable heritage indeed.

Some weights, which look like artistic pill-boxes, have geometric designs. Others illustrate Ashanti proverbs. There are hundreds of Ashanti proverbs, and people use them constantly in conversation to clinch a point or to express in brief the nation's wisdom. They are familiar to every Ashanti, but need explaining to outsiders. One gold weight, for example, shows two men lying on a flat board. The first is lying on his stomach, the second on his back. The proverb is: I am lying on my back and cannot see the sky god. How can you expect to see him lying on your stomach? This proverb probably means that if one cannot understand, it doesn't matter how he tackles a problem. Another gold weight is a tiny board with a head resting on it. It illustrates the proverb: The king sees everything.

Other weights portray people, land animals, fishes, plants, and household objects. Any design could be used. There are figurines of a man with a pipe carrying a basket and a man with a knife carrying burdens on his head. Still another shows a man sacrificing a fowl to the sky god.

To weigh their gold men measured out an amount with a small gold-dust scoop that looked like a spoon. They, too, are shown at the Smithsonian exhibit. Using regular jewelers' scales, a man placed gold weights on one side and the gold dust on the other. To weigh tiny quantities of gold dust people used seeds, grains, and beads.

In addition to the gold weights at the British Museum in London, there are displays of Ashanti gold ornaments. They are fabulous indeed. There are large gold masks, breastplates, bracelets of all sizes and designs, headbands, knee and ankle and saddle ornaments, pins and brooches and rings, canes with gold knobs, fly whisks with gold handles.

Today the Ashanti-owned Ashanti Goldfields Corporation, with headquarters at Kumasi, employs almost as many people as does the entire government of Ghana. The gold ore mined there is the richest in the world and produces an ounce of gold for every ton of earth mined, as compared to some American mines that yield $\frac{1}{10}$ of an ounce of gold for each ton mined.

While searching for new gold deposits,

geologists have also found more diamonds and valuable ores, such as manganese and bauxite. These ores will boost Ghana's income as more mines are opened, industrial plants built, and more electric power becomes available to refine the ores.

Many Ashanti, however, still earn their livelihood by working at the age-old crafts. Craftsmen work in huts and courtyards in their home compounds. There are basket makers, carpenters, who make furniture for the needs of their town, and leatherworkers, who make shoes and sandals. Local people make bricks, pottery, and gold and silver jewelry. Smiths make simple hoes and other farming implements. They even make guns from locally smelted iron or from scrap iron and imported steel.

In the old days the Ashanti made clothing from skins or pounded bark into cloth. Some of their bark cloth was outstanding and is now on display in Ghanaian museums.

Cotton could not be grown in the moist lands of the Ashanti, but when imported cotton yarn became available, their weavers produced a re-

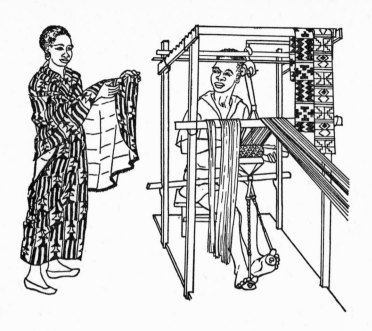

markable cloth called *kente*. They also used silk yarn to make *kente* by unraveling silk material. The looms were very narrow and produced cloth that was only four inches wide, but could be as long as thirty feet. The weavers wove it into bright, colorful, complicated designs. These narrow strips of rich textiles were then sewed artistically into long, wide pieces. The cloth became the formal dress of the Ashanti and is now the traditional Ghanaian dress.

These designs have become so famous that they have been given names and favorite proverbs are associated with them. One *kente* design is called Mamponhemaa. It means queen mother of Mampong. Another design is called Sikafuturo, which means gold dust. As its name implies, this cloth is very expensive, and only the rich and important people can afford it. There is another design called Ebusuaye Dom, meaning a family is an army, a proverb that says there is strength in family unity.

*Kente* is now worn for all formal occasions: meetings, weddings, and parties. When Ghanaians appear in it outside of Ghana at important meetings in Africa, Europe, and America, they stand out from everyone else. With the *kente* outfit, which looks like a Roman toga, Ghanaians wear a bright, handwoven cap and Roman sandals. A woman's *kente* dress looks very much like an Indian sari—a long garment that serves as formal dress and shawl combined.

Modern weavers, who work on broad looms, also use *kente* designs when making bedspreads,

tablecloths, and towels, which tourists are eager
to buy.

Ghana already has some cotton mills whose
output supplements the imported cotton goods.
And more mills will be built as more power becomes available. For this program the government has laid out two- , five- , and seven-year
plans to be accomplished under the Industrial
Development Corporation. The plans also in-
clude the building of factories for making
cigars and cigarettes, for bricks and tiles, and
for machine parts. Despite these future projects,
manufactured goods will not replace for a long
time the home crafts on which the Ashanti depend.

# 8
## THE
## GOLDEN
## HARVEST

The Gold Coast is still a rich region of West Africa, but its name was dropped on March 6, 1957, when its people became independent. Its new name, Ghana, is a very ancient African name for an equally ancient African kingdom that flourished south of the Sahara Desert up to the eleventh century. In July, 1960, the country became the Republic of Ghana and elected its first president, Osagyefo Dr. Kwame Nkrumah, and its parliament for a term of five years. The Ashanti people, however, are still Ashanti first and Ghanaians second. They have their *Asantehene* at Kumasi and their regional chiefs, and village heads, and housefathers, but their roles are constantly changing.

In the past the trade goods that brought about such vital changes in Ashanti history were added comforts but not really essential to the people. The important foods were raised by the Ashanti themselves. Had the trade goods been cut off, the Ashanti would have survived. But without their farming, hunting, and fishing, they could not live. The corn, vegetables, cereals, bananas, sweet potatoes, or yams the women raised were assurance against starvation. Whatever else they earned was a welcome addition to the standard of living. The Ashanti today are still largely farmers, as is some seventy percent of the entire Ghanaian population.

Surprising as it may seem, the current staple food of the West Africans, manioc, was brought from Brazil by the Portuguese about 1600, but did not become widespread till the eighteenth century. We use manioc, which we call tapioca, in puddings. The Ashanti eat it as a cereal called *fufu*.

Yams and plantains, or bananas, are seasoned with peppers, then mashed or cut into chunks for stews and vegetable soups. Their bread or biscuit is called *canky*, and it is made of Indian corn. The corn is first pounded in a large mortar. Then it may be further refined by grinding it between two large stones. The bottom stone is larger and slightly concave. The top one is a stone roller and with it the housewife crushes the kernels. She raises the large stone slightly from the ground, so it slants, and stoops behind it. Moving with the roller, she pushes it back and forth. The ground meal spills to one side, and she sifts it into a basin. When ready to cook, the housewife mixes the cornmeal with water. Sometimes she adds palm wine. The cornmeal may be baked into small cakes. It may also be rolled in banana leaves and baked in small ovens as loaves of bread, which is very tasty.

Tobacco was introduced to the Ashanti by Americans. It was quickly accepted and soon came into common use throughout the region, as it has throughout the world.

Other new crops were the fruit trees, especially citrus fruit, which the Europeans needed to combat scurvy. Lemons, melons, oranges, also tamarind, bananas, and coconuts came from Asia. Pineapple, papaya, and guava came from the Americans, as well as mango, avocado, and sugarcane.

By now these crops have all become native, and the Africans depend on them. They raise them successfully and have enough to sell in town markets for needed cash.

Fish, too, is still important to the Ashanti. Ghana has some 350 miles of coastline, and the coastal people fish a great deal. Today fresh frozen fish is carried inland by trucks. As dams are built more fishing will be available in the rivers and streams.

Today, however, the Ashanti cannot earn a living just by raising food for the household and working at crafts. People need more and more manufactured goods, medicines, better housing, education, and training for this age of technology. For these things an adult has to have a cash income.

Ghana has three major exports, which provide jobs and incomes for its inhabitants. Gold is third on the list, and timber comes next. The most important export—Ghana's real golden harvest—is cocoa. Cocoa accounts for over seventy percent of the total exports, and the Ashanti produce most of it. Each year Ghana exports half a million tons of cocoa to world markets.

The beginnings of this cocoa industry were very inauspicious. They tell in Ghana that a blacksmith from the Gold Coast, named Tetteh Quarshie, traveled south to the island of Fernando Po. There he saw cocoa plantations and learned that they produced a very rich income. Determined to get rich himself, he took back with him in either 1878 or 1879 one cocoa pod, with which he made a start. Others in Ghana add to this story that missionaries had begun as early as 1858 to introduce what they called the chocolate tree to the Gold Coast.

Tetteh Quarshie produced only one tree from his pod. From this tree came more pods and hence more trees. Seeing that they thrived, other people began to import cocoa pods. And so an industry began.

The cocoa tree needs fairly fertile soil, a warm, moist climate, and shade, which is furnished by forest trees. A man starts a cocoa plantation by clearing forest land, planting the cocoa seed or seedlings, and at the same time planting corn, cassava, or bananas, so the young shoots will be protected from the sun. After two or three years of patience and hard work the seedlings need no additional protection other than the high crowns of the forest trees. With care cocoa trees can go on bearing for many, many years.

The common type of cocoa, Amelonado, gives its first small yield only after five years. Its full productiveness begins only after ten years. A better variety of cocoa, called Upper Amazon, discovered in South America along the Amazon River, bears at an earlier age. But this variety is a late comer.

The pods, between six and eight inches in length, grow right on the tree trunk. The main crop of cocoa is harvested between September and January, and a small mid-crop is harvested in May and June. On good farms the yield per acre can be between 1000 and 1200 pounds. Each tree yields about eight pods, a total of half a pound of cocoa. A half pound of cocoa, dried, roasted, exported, refined, and packaged, and put on grocery shelves costs thirty-nine cents at our local supermarket.

Before the cocoa beans can be exported the

farmer and his family put in more labor. He and his family carefully split the pods. The sticky pulp has to be removed from the beans. The beans are then covered and allowed to ferment for about six days. It is during this fermentation process that the chocolate flavor develops in the beans. Next the fermented beans are carefully dried. If not properly dried, the beans become moldy.

At the market the beans are examined by professional graders, who sample them and grade

them into four categories. After inspection the beans are put into sacks, sealed, and stamped. The stamp is from the Agricultural Produce Marketing Board that maintains standards for its products. Ghanaian cocoa is rated very highly in the world's markets. Licensed buyers of cocoa today are the farmers' cooperative societies. The Marketing Board sets a uniform price on cocoa for all Ghanaian farmers. It sells the cocoa abroad and keeps part of the income for development, for research, for Ghanaian scholarships and for hospitals. Ghana also has cocoa processing plants but it needs more. One plant today produces 20,000 tons of cocoa. Whenever there is an overproduction of cocoa, some of it has to be dumped, so as not to put too much cocoa on the market and thus lower its price. If there were more processing plants in Ghana, this cocoa might be processed before it is dumped. Then it could be used by the people rather than destroyed.

A few years ago the cocoa industry was threatened by diseases. Various insect pests attack the cocoa trees. The most feared is a disease called swollen root, which is caused by female mealybugs. However, with intensive research, continuous spraying, and watchfulness, the industry has been saved from this danger. At one time a half million infected trees had to be cut down to prevent the swollen root from spreading.

The Ashanti, as well as the rest of the Ghanaian cocoa farmers, cooperate fully in the spraying program. But they are unhappy that the Agricultural Produce Marketing Board pays them such a low price for the cocoa. Should the crop fail in any one year, the Marketing Board would help tide the farmers over till the next crop can be marketed. The independent Ashanti farmers, however, feel they are fully capable of setting funds aside themselves against such emergencies. They want to be paid in full for the cocoa they sell. They themselves would then contribute to scholarships, to building roads and harbors through taxes. The Ashanti have always managed for themselves, and they feel they could manage now. Some cocoa producers of the other regions join the Ashanti in this attitude. They further object to the control the Marketing Board has over the number of trees a farmer is permitted to plant.

So long as there are such differences within a country, there are bound to be conflicts. In 1955 the Ashanti and some of their neighbors proclaimed that they were being treated unfairly by the government. They and their allies formed a National Liberation Council and demanded that a federal system of states and a two-party system be established in Ghana.

These demands brought riots and terror before they were suppressed by the government.

The central government believes that Ghana is not yet ready for a two-party system. The Ashanti claim that the one-party system denies them a voice in their government, which they have always had. According to Ashanti tradition, anyone can be heard before a judge. They were, therefore, appalled when their lawyers were prohibited from defending them and were jailed instead. The ruling party under President Kwame Nkrumah, the C.P.P. (Convention People's Party), called all opposition treason and treated opponents as traitors. Ashanti leaders and others were then jailed without trial.

Another problem facing the Ashanti is that their traditional inheritance customs are not suitable for men who own cocoa fields. It is the custom that a nephew inherits the wealth and property of his uncle. A man's cocoa fields, however, are cared for by himself, his wife, and his children. He, therefore, feels that the property should be inherited upon his death by his wife, sons, and daughters and not by his nephews and nieces, who have not worked for him. If a man can, he wills, before witnesses, that his property should go to his own family. But when a man dies without such a witnessed statement, his nephews get the property. The Ashanti are anxious to change this age-old custom.

The same problem troubles other landowners. Only members of the same clan can inherit land. The sons, who belong to a different clan from their father, may own the trees on the land willed to them, but not the land itself. This division leads to disputes over land and tree planting.

Close family ties were essential when people lived and worked in small villages. They shared their produce, their compounds, and were ruled by the head of the household. Nowadays, however, young people go to live and work in big cities. Their homes are small and rents are high. They just barely manage on their low wages, since everything in a town has to be bought for cash. Clothing is very expensive, and the Ashanti like to dress well. When visiting clansmen arrive, therefore, they are received with dismay. The young people have no extra room for them, nor can they afford to feed and entertain them for any length of time, as they would in their own village. Yet relations expect hospitality. Many young people, consequently, keep their whereabouts in town a secret to avoid such embarrassing and disastrous visits. This behavior tends to estrange families and relations. Customs will have to change to accommodate modern social situations.

People say this tribalism should be abolished. But such a change is not easy. There are many good things that tribalism offers its people. Changes have to be made, but they should come slowly and be studied well, so as to let the people keep important roots and family connections that are essential to all of us.

Industrialization is progressing, in the meantime, with ever greater speed. The Ghanaians hope it will hit full stride now that the giant Volta River hydroelectric project and dam are completed. They are located at Akosombo, some forty miles inland from the modern harbor of Tema. Already a large aluminum plant, being built there, expects to absorb half of the electric power output. The remainder will be used for industrial and agricultural development. This undertaking will bring further prosperity to the Ashanti, too.

Kumasi, today, is a prosperous busy city of a quarter of a million people. Still the Ashanti's capital, it is rich and colorful and has earned the name Garden City because of its abundance of trees and flower gardens. Kumasi's streets are always filled with people, who come from all over Africa. Some are dressed in European clothes; others wear colorful, cool cotton togas. Women still carry loads on their head, and their babies rest snugly on their back. Tall buildings, more warehouses along the railroad yard, movie houses, and schools are being built. The Kwame Nkrumah University of Science and Technology is located in Kumasi. Cocoa and timber trucks continuously load and unload in town, for Kumasi is a railroad center as well as the main exchange for gold and diamonds. The African Manganese Company has its headquarters at Kumasi for the Nsuta Manganese Mines.

The famous marketplace of Kumasi still sprawls over several acres in the center of town, supplying the city with everything it needs. The tiny shops swarm with buyers. People meet, bargain, and talk. Ashanti boys become traders at a very early age. They weave in and out of the crowds and traffic shouting their wares. The important fresh foods on which Kumasi housewives depend—yams, maize, tomatoes, beans, peanuts, peppers, and fruit—are still brought to town by village women and spread out in attractive patterns to entice buyers. There are special sections where live chickens, sheep, goats, and cows can be bought. There are also sections for manufactured goods, for pots and pans, furniture, radios, *kente* cloth in silk and cotton, and bookstores.

The story of the Ashanti might have been very different but for the gold found on their lands and the slave trade. With the wealth that came from trading they were able to conquer and expand. All this power has now passed into

history. What the Ashanti have left today are the basic things that have enabled them to survive and to call themselves a great people—now almost a million strong. They have retained their family life. They have their own language and literature, their religion and local government. They are still hard-working, independent farmers, craftsmen, and traders. To such a people the future is bound to be kind.

# INDEX